AFTER DEATH?

Other books by David L. Edwards available from Cassell:

What Anglicans Believe New Edition (1999)
Christianity: The First Two Thousand Years (1997)
What Is Catholicism? (1994)

AFTER DEATH?

Past beliefs and real possibilities

David L. Edwards

CASSELL

Cassell
Wellington House
125 Strand
London WC2R 0BB

370 Lexington Avenue
New York
NY 10017–6550

www.cassell.co.uk

First published 1999

British Library Cataloguing-in-Publication Data
A catalogue record for this book is available from the British Library.

ISBN 0-304-70458-X

Typeset by Kenneth Burnley, Wirral, Cheshire.
Printed and bound in Great Britain by Creative Print and Design Wales, Ebbw Vale.

Contents

Preface

THIS IS A SMALLISH BOOK about a great human question. We are all going to die, and as far as we can see all of what we are will die: will anything of us survive? And this question is at the heart of what we mean when we ask what life means. We all think about this, often from an early age but more intensely as our time runs out (my own last birthday was my seventieth). All through history, societies and their cultures – in particular their religions and philosophies – have done what they could to guide and sustain people as they have moved towards this destination and as they have mourned, but in societies which are in some sense modern, and therefore in some sense secular, this official sort of comfort has quite recently become less accessible. Many things which in the past have been taught with some authority and believed with some assurance have become incredible to most of the kind of people who may come across this book. Much of what has been taught in the religious institutions seems plainly wrong and much of what has been believed by the public seems merely sentimental. So I have written for readers who want to think for themselves and in all honesty.

Although I hope I may reach and interest some readers who do not share my nationality, I have been influenced by the British experience. Scepticism, agnosticism or sheer confusion must often have been the human response to the devastation and the enigma of death, but in Britain the acceptance of the churches' traditional doctrines and customs has been reduced at an extraordinary speed during the twentieth century, and this change has been accompanied by a revolution in how we usually die and in how the survivors dispose of our bodies. Yet the clergy continue to be prominent in most funerals and bits of the Bible continue to help in bereavement, even if they are now fading memories. Therefore as a priest of the Church of England I have felt a special obligation to think out afresh what may be true about death and what may be real possibilities about life after death.

What can we believe now, if we want nothing but the truth? What light has been shed by the 'parapsychology' of modern investigators and by the many recent reports of near-death experiences? Shall we 'see' the dead whom we love? What, if anything, are our 'souls'? Are they naturally immortal? Did they exist before our present lives? Will they return to earth in new bodies? And what real possibility may there be in old beliefs about the 'resurrection of the body'? Did Jesus rise from the dead and, if he did, was his resurrection physical? What is still believable about hell? Or about purgatory? Or about heaven?

In struggling to respond to such questions, which have been my own questions as well as the public's, I have considered (however superficially) many beliefs which have been expressed in the past, including the beliefs of the great world religions, but the reader will find without surprise that when trying to find answers I have paid most attention to the tradition to which I belong – the Christian tradition. Light has come to me through the Bible and through the Church of many ages, although that is not to say that I have finished up adhering to any kind of fundamentalism. In this book I conclude that it is a real possibility for us to be given, after our deaths, one by one as continuing personalities, a share in the eternal life of God – which to me is the meaning of the resurrection for which Christians hope. This future is possible solely because of God, as was shown with a unique power in the life of Jesus, including his death and what followed his death. This conclusion may seem remarkably simple after the large and profound debate which I have not ignored, but the truth can be simple. And of course I am not the first person to reach this conclusion. But what is true need not be completely new.

In recent years there has been much good writing in this field – sociological and philosophical, anthropological and historical, medical and literary, psychological and parapsychological, and theological. Because it has been my ambition to provide a concise summary of the main themes in this literature rather than offer an academic work, I have not included footnotes. But at the end I give a list of more than a hundred books to which I am indebted. Because there may be a wish to check my interpretations, I have given references to the Bible and other scriptures, but I have not stuck to any one translation. Quite often I have felt it unavoidable to use 'man' or 'he' without meaning 'men' exclusively, and without hinting that God is male, but I offer apologies for this usage if it seems offensive. I am deeply grateful for the advice of Peter Jupp, who in addition to many other contributions to this difficult subject is co-editor of the journal *Mortality*. And once again I offer thanks for three indispensables: the support of my wife Sybil, the availability of the Cambridge University Library, and the encouragement of my publishers.

DAVID L. EDWARDS
Winchester, Spring 1999

1
Where We Are

MANY CENTURIES AGO Confucius asked Chi Lu: 'When you do not understand life, how can you understand death?' The force of this question has increased now that we do understand more about life, particularly about its physical basis. Can anything importantly true be said about death except that we die?

Sometimes the question about the Grim Reaper is asked casually and answered flippantly, yet the joking response may be anxiously defensive. Sometimes adolescents and even children are fascinated by the end which seems to them a long way off, wondering whether people become as dead as pets. Sometimes the question is answered almost as soon as it is asked, for a tradition inherited or adopted comes to the rescue with a firm reassurance; yet when we are being honest we have to confess to anxiety, ignorance and uncertainty. Then we know that we have to think again about a mystery where, it seems, everything has been said and nothing has been proved. Sometimes the pain in the question is dulled by entertainment, yet it is a fact of modern life that while it has become very unlikely that a member of the family will be dying in a bedroom upstairs, a fictional, violent death may well be the centrepiece in the living-room, for in TV dramas (as in novels) a death, or the danger of one, is very often thought essential if the plot is to grab attention. The situation has not changed much since the American Academy of Pediatrics was told in 1971 that the average was 18,000 killings on TV viewed by the age of 14. And sometimes the platitude that we all must die is thrown at me. Perhaps I know more sharply than usual that I must die (soon?). Perhaps I am bereaved. Perhaps someone famous – who has seemed close to me through the media – dies and we are reminded that we are all passengers on the *Titanic.*

Many mourners in Britain in recent years have been comforted by hearing or reading a small part of a sermon preached by a distinguished clergyman of the Church of England in 1910. Probably no part of any sermon preached in twentieth-century Britain has had more influence. Henry Scott Holland expressed what he thought 'we seem to feel' when 'we look down upon the quiet face' of 'one who has been very near and dear to us'. 'What the face says in its sweet silence' is, he suggested, this:

> Death is nothing at all . . . I have only slipped away into the next room. Nothing has happened. Everything remains exactly as it was. I am I, and you are you, and the old life which we lived together so fondly is untouched, unchanged . . . Wear no false air of solemnity or sorrow. Laugh as we always laughed at the little jokes that we enjoyed together. Play, smile, think of me, pray for me . . . All is well. Nothing is hurt; nothing is lost. One brief moment and all will be as it was before. How we shall laugh at the trouble of parting when we meet again!

But in the same sermon Scott Holland spoke of another possible response to death. Understandably, this passage is never used at funerals.

> There is the familiar and instinctive recoil from death as embodying the supreme and irrevocable disaster . . . It makes all we do here meaningless and empty . . . It is so inexplicable, so ruthless, so blundering, this death that we must die. It is the cruel ambush into which we are snared. It is the pit of destruction. It wrecks, it defeats, it shatters.

This preacher knew without any escapism

> the long, horrible silence that follows when we become aware of what we have lost out of our daily intercourse by the withdrawal of the immediate presence . . . We shall find it impossible to keep at the high level without a word, without a sign, to reassure us of its truth . . . Once again the old terror will come down upon us . . . It is all blind, dismal, unutterable darkness. We grope in vain . . . Not a sound comes back! Not a cry reaches us! Dumb! Dumb as the night, that terrifying silence!

Scott Holland expounded what he believed about the mystery of death elsewhere, but it is suggestive that in this sermon preached on

Whit Sunday in 1910 he did not attempt to speak with enthusiasm about the 'communion of saints'. One reason was that he was preaching on the Sunday after the death of King Edward VII. He referred to the 'irreparable disaster of a death which had touched the very heart of our national life' but he must have known, as the congregation listening knew, that the king had not lived as a saint. It was difficult to imagine His Majesty being carried immediately from his deathbed to the glories of heaven as traditionally pictured. But it was out of the question to say that the worldliness of his character had already been punished by imprisonment in the never-ending torture chambers of the traditional hell, and it would also have been tactless to open up the question whether Protestants could make any use of the picture inherited by Catholics from the Middle Ages of 'purgatory' as a painful preparation for heaven.

In the summer of 1997 there was another very public connection between royalty and death, creating a period of mourning and a funeral which dramatically exposed realities in British public opinion and which fascinated many millions who watched TV or read newspapers outside Britain. The world's response made this the largest involvement in any funeral in history. It was not an expression of shock after the sudden death of a leader who had wielded great power and embodied great promises, a kind of mourning which naturally brings to mind the murder of President Kennedy in 1963. This funeral was a confused response to the violent death of a symbol of emotional realities deeper than politics. Nor was it entirely like the death of a star of entertainment, sport or fashion. The central figure had been the most photographed woman in the world, but many reactions to the tragedy of her death arose from depths which no camera could penetrate.

The car crash which killed Diana, Princess of Wales, was followed by an outpouring of grief which was fed by the media but which was plainly and painfully sincere. The media responded to emotions which few of those whose business it was to symbolize, or express or study, public opinion had expected to be so intense and so widespread. Genuine grief brought seas of flowers at the gates of palaces, messages and tributes left in churches and other centres of mourning, the closure of shops and a silence broken only by sobs in the streets of London. As the hearse drove to her grave in the grounds of her childhood home amid flowers and applause, it was a kind of coronation. But the Princess was praised not chiefly for her beauty and glamour but for her compassion and her ability to make emotional contact quickly, opening herself to people trapped in suffering – and she was praised because she had herself suffered much and had made this the material of her spiritual victory.

In all these ways the mourning was well within the Christian tradition. But it seems possible that many who showed their grief in public – indeed, in large crowds – did so with such feeling partly because this was a rare occasion on which such an open expression of natural emotions was permitted and even encouraged. It is certain that many of those who mourned were unfamiliar with the historic churches' doctrines and ceremonics and that the Princess for whom they grieved had herself not relied on traditional forms of the Christian religion. In her distress she had consulted a variety of 'alternative' therapists, including an astrologer. Her funeral did not follow any order in regular use and there was no sermon. Although the scene was traditional and the service in Westminster Abbey included old words and music, the 'programme' (as TV commentators called it) was specially devised. The parts which made the most impact on the public were the lament for a 'candle in the wind' sung by Elton John and the indignantly heartfelt address delivered from the pulpit by her brother. Both were applauded, in a further breach with the conventions. Sorrow and anger were the most prominent elements, rather than any Christian assurance about resurrection and eternal life, since a nation where orthodoxy had been shattered felt it to be a time for honesty. The church authorities deserved, and won, praise for recognizing this. Diana belonged to an established order of society and of ideology: born into the aristocracy, married into the Royal Family, adored by the public, blessed in her baptism, wedding and funeral by the Church of England. But her life and her death stirred so many feelings because she had been conspicuously insecure and vulnerable.

That eruption of grief in 1997 came from a nation where, according to a number of recent surveys of public opinion, no more than half of the population believes with assurance in any kind of life after death. The other half either refuses to say more than 'don't know' or else is fairly confident that death is completely the end of a human life. Inevitably those proportions of belief, complete indecision and unbelief are less precise than is the fact that about 600,000 people die in Britain each year (more than half of them over the age of 75). Sometimes it seems that more people than this half believe in 'life after death', sometimes that fewer do, and often that everybody ought to be among the 'Don't know's. And, inevitably, concise answers cannot cover the whole range of thoughts and feelings. But probably these rough figures do convey a reliable impression. The numbers of firm believers in life after death seem to be significantly lower in Britain than in the USA or in most of the Two-thirds World, although they are significantly higher than those reported from Japan or some other European countries.

An attractive feature of this situation is that many people are being honest as they face a searching question about themselves and those they love. But perhaps more open to criticism is the fact that many people in Britain still arrange funerals involving a 'minister of religion' who is probably a stranger, and using religious language which expresses doctrines perhaps not sincerely accepted, perhaps not taken seriously, either by the mourners or by the deceased. Britain is not alone here: in Sweden only five per cent of the population attend church on Sundays and under 40 per cent tell pollsters that they believe in life after death, but some 90 per cent of the funerals are conducted by the Lutheran clergy. Any fair criticism must be made remembering that all through history people have used the customs of the local religion – 'myths' and 'rituals' would be the words (meant to be neutral) used by sociologists and anthropologists – to provide some reaffirmation or rebirth of life in a crisis such as death. It would be obviously wrong, because utterly insensitive, to expect mourners to pass some kind of theological examination before being allowed to gain access to the religious traditions in their inheritance. But it seems less objectionable to regret that when a death has sharpened up sensitivity to the ultimate reality of the human existence it may meet a formal response which does not voice the deepest feelings. The anthropologist Maurice Bloch has observed that it is the purpose of funerary traditions to fight back after apparent defeat and to dramatize the 'rebounding conquest' of death. A conquest must involve a real battle with real satisfaction for the victors, who now feel themselves to be, in Bloch's phrase, 'the hunter not the prey'. Unless this need can be met by the teachers and representatives of religion, in a country such as Britain the spread of non-religious, or at least non-standard, funerals may be rapid (and may be encouraged by the publicity for the unconventional elements in Princess Diana's funeral).

What guidance is offered by the leaders of thought?

In *How the Mind Works* (1997) Steven Pinker, a brilliant American science-based thinker, indicated that one of the few puzzles which cause him a moment's hesitation is the prominence of religion in the history of humankind. He wrote: 'The common answer – that people take comfort in the thought of a benevolent shepherd, a universal plan, or an afterlife – is unsatisfactory, because it only raises the question of *why* a mind would evolve to find comfort in beliefs it can plainly see are false'. The explanation which he prefers is that 'religion is a desperate measure which people resort to when the stakes are high and they have exhausted the usual techniques for the causation of success'.

It might be thought that this brisk identification of religion with magic would be recognized by philosophers as not an entirely adequate assessment of the history of religion, particularly as people with complicated emotions confront the ancient and mysterious ideas that God is real and that death is somehow survived. But *The Oxford Dictionary of Philosophy* (1994) was compiled by Simon Blackburn, who after teaching philosophy in Oxford for 21 years and editing the prestigious journal *Mind* had become a professor in the University of North Carolina. Mentioning belief in personal immortality, he saw a simple alternative. The belief, he wrote, 'may involve only the survival of our "soul" understood as an immaterial (non-physical) thinking substance contingently (not necessarily) and temporarily lodged in our present body'. No argument in favour of the soul thus understood 'enjoys much respect among contemporary philosophers' (because of modern knowledge that the personality depends on the body and the mind depends on the brain). We are also told that the only alternative to belief in the immortality of the soul is belief in the resurrection of the body, here defined as the claim that 'a person could return to life after dying, either with his or her original body or with a new one'. Each belief 'raises severe problems of personal identity' (for how could a resurrected 'I' be the same 'I' as the person who died, perhaps a long time ago, in a body which has perished, or how could I have been a member of an Indian family unconnected with my own, or a person who used to live in China or Ancient Egypt?). No other idea about life after death is considered by Blackburn – which seems a pity, since there is another idea and it deserves to be taken seriously. Because elephants are neither pink nor blue it does not follow that there are no elephants.

No belief in God as the giver of immortality is taken seriously in this *Dictionary of Philosophy*. It is acknowledged that 'special revelation and faith remain the most powerful sources of belief in immortality' but Blackburn is among those who firmly reject 'the supernatural nature of the claim being made'. Does the claim rest on experience? No, for 'the theory which comes with religious experience seems untestable and devoid of any except doubtful emotional significance'. Does God make immortality possible? No, for 'once a description of a Supreme Being is hit upon, there remains the problem of providing any reason for supposing that anything exists answering to that description'. Is it possible that there will be 'a final arena in which the just triumph and the unjust are punished'? No, for such claims are 'more like wishful thinking than arguments'.

Perhaps more telling than any of these arguments is the fact that Professor Blackburn did not think that his readers would expect him to defend them at any length. It may seem not enough to say that religion, being emotional, is 'doubtful', for so is love; or to say that belief in God presents problems, for so does the belief that the universe is ultimately a complete accident; or to say that a hope is 'wishful', because we all have our hopes which are wishes. But this *Dictionary* seems to be designed for readers to whom these objections are not likely to occur.

Such is the change in the climate of opinion, in Britain at any rate, since the days when Joseph Butler, a respected philosopher as well as a bishop, could expect some agreement with the claim that 'whether we are to live in a future state, as it is the most important question which can possibly be asked, so it is the most intelligible which can be expressed in language'. In the next, more troubled century, Dostoyevsky, who may be the greatest of all novelists who have seen into the human heart, claimed: 'There is only one supreme idea on earth, the immortality of the human soul; all other profound ideas by which people live are only an extension of it.' When in Plato's *Phaedo* Socrates is teaching his version of immortality, he asks Cebes: 'Is not philosophy the study of death?' He expects the answer he gets: 'Certainly.' Professor Blackburn shows a great respect for Plato ('many would claim that the depth and range of his thought have never been surpassed'), and for Hegel ('he continues to be a focal point for many thinkers'). Hegel thought that 'history is the record of what humanity does about death'. Two lines in the poetry of W. B. Yeats are specially haunting:

> Man is in love and loves what vanishes,
> What more is there to say?[1]

But Yeats answered his own question. He was fascinated by death and by the possibility that something does not die utterly. And so he said a lot.

Much in the history of religion is summed up by the famous prayer in the Hindu Upanishads: 'Lead me from the unreal to the real! Lead me from death to immortality!' As a voice from America, William James ended his *Varieties of Religious Experience* (1902) with a pardonable exaggeration: 'Religion, in fact, for the great majority of our own race, *means* immortality, and nothing else. God is the producer of immortality; and whoever has doubts of immortality is written down as an atheist without further trial.' Innumerable words about heaven have in the past held out promises of joys far greater than anything known in this life, or anything which can be described or imagined, when at last the meaning and fulfilment of this mysterious and often tragic life would be made known not in 'success' but in the triumph of justice (not merely of 'the just') and of love. The way to heaven would lie through many fears, dangers and ordeals for which the traditional images have been the night without a path, the dark wood, the jungle, the marsh, the desert, the very high mountain, the wide, cold river, the forbidding walls and the difficult gateway. Much suffering before, during or after death might be needed to rebuke, punish, purge or cure the sins of this life after temptations by the world, the flesh and the devil. For the great religions coming out of India the road to the ultimate bliss must lie through many lives on earth, but even the Buddhist's Nirvana, 'No-thing-ness', has been reckoned infinitely desirable. For religions able to imagine glory more concretely, heaven has been seen in 'the heavens', far beyond the stars but shining in a splendour greater than theirs; or, coming more or less down to earth, it has been pictured as a harbour or island in a sea, or as a river of fresh water in a dry land, or as a city, a temple, a royal court, a first-class restaurant, a meadow or a garden, with jewels, gold, flowers, fruits, perfumes, maidens, angels, music or sheer peace and light, beautiful 'as a bride adorned for her husband'.

There is abundant evidence that hopes of heaven have given comfort and strength to millions upon millions of people amid their distress in this life. Karl Marx regarded the attentive criticism of religion as vitally important because these illusions had been like a dream induced by opium, making impossible the anger and the determination needed to change history by making a revolution. But that great materialist, acknowledging the emotional power of the dream, called religion's hope of heaven the 'heart of a heartless world'. Charles Darwin, whom Marx venerated, regarded the rejection of religious fundamentalism as vitally important because it was the enemy of the true knowledge which can be acquired, however painfully, by research, study, thought and courage. But he did not publish his discovery of evolution by natural selection for twenty years, and he suffered from a prolonged nervous illness, because he knew well what people felt. A frequent reaction was that there could be no God and no heaven for the descendants of apes. He was happily married to a devout Christian and he supported the village church, although not with his regular attendance. In his ignorant youth he had intended to become a clergyman like many of those who taught him. He remembered the world ruled by God as a preparation for eternity.

As the fourth Christian century became the fifth, Augustine, Bishop of Hippo, had an influence larger than the average emperor's because he saw the vision so clearly. 'Our hope is the resurrection of the dead,' he said in a sermon. 'Our faith is the resurrection of the dead. It is also our love, because the preaching of "things not seen" inflames us and arouses in us a longing for those things . . . If faith in the resurrection of the dead is taken away, all Christian doctrine perishes.' England's first historian, Bede, thought that he was pointing to the strongest attraction of Christianity for the pagan Anglo-Saxons when he told the story of a nobleman who advised King Edwin that the missionary ought to be heard because he might throw some light on death. Otherwise human life seemed to be like the flight of a bird through a hall lit for a feast on a winter's evening: the bird flutters from darkness to darkness. And not many years passed before (according to Bede) another man of Northumbria, Drythelm, the father of a family, became a hermit because, while believed to be dead, in a dream he visited both heaven and hell.

In 1650 Richard Baxter published a classic, *The Saints' Everlasting Rest.* He intended 'but the length of a sermon or two' since the only book within his reach was the Bible, but he wrote some 800,000 words. He had an excuse for his verbosity since he was ill and deeply depressed during the English civil wars and he thought that his own death was near: 'I began to contemplate more seriously on the Everlasting Rest when I apprehended myself to be on the borders of it.' He admitted that death was a mystery, 'but if I stay until I clearly know, I shall not come again to speak . . . Therefore I will speak while I may, that little, very little which I do know of it.' And he spoke at such length because he felt that the communication of what he knew was urgent. The heaven which God offered would be 'that good which containeth all other good in it' but many were deaf to the offer. So 'this is your time. Now or Never!' Hell was a possibility but the danger of hell was not the main consideration. 'Is it a small thing in thine eyes to be beloved of God?'

We need not go back to remote ages if we are to find a competent philosopher with an open mind about the possibilities that something in people can survive death and that something which people call 'God' is real. Some philosophers still teaching have this attitude, but we may take as an example C. D. Broad, the Cambridge professor whose book of 1925 on *The Mind and its Place in Nature* remains a classic.

In his *Lectures on Psychical Research* (1962) Broad showed a patient interest in claims that 'psychical' (mental and spiritual) realities had been discovered by investigating 'paranormal' (beside the normal) events which as yet could not be explained by any of the sciences, and he stated his conclusion.

> In the known relevant and normal facts there is nothing to suggest, and much to counter-suggest, the possibility of any kind of persistence of the psychical aspect of a human being after the death of his body. On the other hand there are many quite well attested paranormal phenomena which strongly suggest such a persistence, and a few which strongly suggest the full blown survival of a human

> personality. The result is naturally a state of hesitation and scepticism . . . I think I may say that for my part I should be slightly more annoyed than surprised if I should find myself persisting after the death of my present body. One can only wait and see, or alternatively (which is no less likely) wait and not see.

Broad was more impressed by the history of religion. In *Religion, Philosophy and Psychical Research* (1953) he observed that religious and mystical experiences, a fertile source of the belief in the survival of the human personality,

> occur among peoples of different races and social traditions and that they have occurred at all periods of history. I am prepared to admit that, although the experiences have differed considerably at different times and places and although the interpretations of them have differed still more, there are probably certain characteristics which are common to them all and suffice to distinguish them from all other kinds of experience. I think that in view of this it is more likely than not that in religious and mystical experiences men come into contact with some Reality or aspect of Reality which they do not come into contact with in any other way.

One factor in the decline of belief in life after death – 'the eclipse of eternity' – has been the unusual degree of the agnosticism or definite unbelief which some of the most thoughtful and eminent teachers of religion have made public. This honest doubt or unbelief has been noticeable in the modern history of Christian theology. Its abandonment of many past beliefs can be dismissed as heresy but it seems more sensible to say that these sceptics, belonging to a profession often identified in history with dogmatism, and talking the 'theology' which is often used as another word for unimportant nonsense, have deserved their serious audience. Certainly in this book their positions will not be disregarded.

Friedrich Schleiermacher, the founder of modern Protestant theology as the nineteenth century began, wrote that 'in the midst of finitude to be one with the Infinite and in every moment to be eternal: that is the immortality of religion'. In a private letter to the widow he married he explained: 'This is the greatest certainty: . . . there is no death, no perishing of the spirit . . . But the individual's life does not essentially belong to the spirit: it is only an appearance.

We do not know how this appearance is repeated; we can form no conception of it, only poetic visions.'

Schleiermacher, who had the feeling of 'absolute dependence' on the Infinite at the centre of his being, thought that 'for every Christian the only essential thing in every conception he may form of "existence after death" is the persistent union of believers with the Redeemer'. But Rudolf Bultmann, the best-known New Testament scholar in the twentieth century, took a step further. He was convinced that although a death can be 'the final triumph of authenticity' yet 'there is no beyond *after* death, only a beyond *above* death', for there is no personal survival. This conviction was in keeping with his interpretation of the death of Jesus: the life which it summed up and ended caused the disciples to have visions, thus their faith arose in the 'saving efficacy of the cross' while Jesus himself did not 'rise' in any straightforward sense. As Bultmann's disciple Willi Marxsen put it bluntly, '"Jesus is risen" simply means: today the crucified Jesus is calling us to believe.'

Paul Tillich, one of the most influential theologians of the twentieth century, maintained that 'eternal life means that the joy of today has a non-temporal meaning'. Like Bultmann he rejected the idea of 'the endless continuation of a stream of consciousness' and on at least one occasion said that it provided a good description of hell. Like Bultmann he believed that even in death a person is 'known eternally beyond past and future' – known, as he put it, by the 'Ground of Being'. But this knowledge is only the 'essentialization or elevation of the positive into Eternal Life': it is not the love of the eternal God for an individual who will almost certainly need to change after death because before death that individual's life has not been entirely 'positive'. And although Tillich often taught that awareness of the 'Ground of Being' gives to the individual before death the 'courage to be', biographies record that he felt a lifelong anxiety about his own death and believed the prospect of death to be the ground of all other anxieties. 'Since every day a little of our life is taken from us – since we are dying every day – the final hour when we cease to exist does not of itself bring death: it merely completes the dying process.' Tillich's sermon which provided the title of *The Eternal Now* (1963) began: 'It is our destiny and the destiny of everything in our world that we must come to an end.' He said that 'praying means elevating oneself to the eternal' but he maintained that any hope for 'life after death' was 'foolish, wishful thinking'. Like Bultmann he taught that, although we may speak of the eternal in images taken from time, 'there is not eternity *after* time but there is eternity *above* time' – not including personal survival.

In *Death: Meaning and Morality in Contemporary Christian Culture* (1969) a less famous American religious thinker, Milton McGatch, expressed his convictions in words which may seem clearer because they did not come from the German philosophical backgrounds of Bultmann and Tillich. 'Literally conceived', he wrote,

> the idea of an afterlife has no place, makes no sense, and is inconsistent within the framework of the contemporary world-picture. Christians should not try to force themselves to conceive what is inconceivable in their world. We must speak of immortality and resurrection not as facts but as modes of approach to life . . . The mode of resurrection calls upon man to live hard and well and boldly here and now, and to understand that what he does is important in the historical continuum. The mode of immortality calls upon man to concern himself above all with his inner or mental or spiritual development and to regard his place in history as of secondary concern.

In his widely noticed *Death and Immortality* (1970), D. Z. Phillips, a British philosopher who has thought long and hard about religion, was 'at a loss to know what it means to talk of surviving death'. But he suggested that 'eternal life is the reality of goodness, that in terms of which human life is assessed', so that 'speculations about continued existence after death are beside the point'. He acknowledged that this interpretation of eternal life is unlikely to satisfy people who remember what robust encouragement, warning or comfort was given when the idea of 'eternal life' was connected with 'continued existence after death'. So he maintained that a specifically religious value could be attached to good lives before death.

> I am suggesting that eternal life for the believer is participating in the life of God, and that this life has to do with dying to the self, seeing that all things are a gift of God, nothing is ours by right or necessity . . . In learning by contemplation, attention, renunciation, what forgiving, thanking, loving, etc., mean in these

> contexts, the believer is participating in the reality of God; this is what we mean by God's reality.

Both McGatch and Phillips mean by the 'we' who agree with them people who would not regard God as 'the most real thing' (a definition used in the Middle Ages) but would prefer to use this word to recommend a human lifestyle. And some theologians, without sharing that non-realist view of God, have shared the reluctance to let religion speak about eternity. An exposition of the ancient Apostles' Creed to the intelligent laity was provided by Nicholas Lash, a Cambridge professor of theology and a Roman Catholic (*Believing Three Ways in One God*, 1992). When he came to the creed's insistence on 'the resurrection of the body and the life everlasting', he acknowledged that 'it may be understandable that in our nervous curiosity . . . we should seek to peer or speculate beyond the boundary of death, to wonder what "eternal life" is like. Yet all such speculation is, of course, quite futile for we have, and can have, no idea.' Lash therefore recommended 'simply trusting God'. He did not condemn 'imagery which, as it were, wears its metaphorical status on its sleeve' such as imagery in the Bible, but he insisted that the purpose of such imagery is 'to point us to the *present*'.

When leading modern theologians have shown these varying degrees of disquiet about traditional beliefs in life after death, it is clear that a problem has arisen for the Christian religion (at least). Indeed, in *The Beginning and the End of 'Religion'* (1996) Lash made the point himself: while the Christian hope must take time 'deadly seriously' (he wrote a fine study of Marxism as a reminder to Christians of their duties within history), and also must acknowledge to the full the tragedies in time, yet 'the Christian heart is set beyond this time, beyond the edge of time, towards the dawning of eternity'. His motive in being sceptical about images of eternity is indicated when he calls 'the purification of desire' the heart of Christian discipleship, but the desire for eternity, if it can be purified, is finally affirmed.

In his first letter to Corinth (15:12–19) St Paul declared that if there is 'no resurrection of the dead' then 'your preaching is empty and your faith is empty' so that 'we deserve to be pitied more than anyone else'. An American sociologist, Peter Berger, is the author of *The Social Reality of Religion*, published in Britain in 1967.

When originally published in the USA his book had the title *The Sacred Canopy* because it explored the whole of the 'canopy' which religion has erected over human life, over individuals and their societies. But Berger argued that 'every human society is, in the last resort, men banded together in the face of death' and he concluded that 'the power of religion depends, in the last resort, upon the credibility of the banners it puts into the hands of men as they stand before death or, more accurately, walk towards it'. More recently a British sociologist of religion, Douglas Davies, concluded a world-wide survey of *Death, Ritual and Belief* (1997) with the observation that 'the extent to which a religion is capable of facing death and giving people, both as individuals and as a community, a sense of transcending mortality, is the extent to which that religion will flourish'.

Banners protesting against death can seem to be no more than invitations to escapism from the reality of the present, but in the history of religion they have been carried in a spirit more resembling the seriousness of a demonstration by protesters who are well aware of the ugly reality of what concerns them. Death is hated as the climax of what is evil in the experienced world. It does not seem to have been the case that the origins of religion lay solely in the fear of death: recently, scholars have almost all agreed that the truth, so far as it can be found, is far more complicated. This is indicated by the fact that in many languages there is no word equivalent to 'religion': religion is what a community does in togetherness, what an individual does in solitariness, what is thought or felt or danced in response to life as a whole with its natural and supernatural backgrounds. Religion can be traditional or charismatic, authoritarian or rebellious. But religion certainly has challenged death and has done so with the greatest prospect of credibility when it has not taken the problem lightly. In 1850 Tennyson published *In Memoriam*, condensing the whole crisis of religious faith which many sensitive Victorians experienced into his grief for a dead friend. In 1961 C. S. Lewis adopted the name of N. W. Clerk in order to publish *A Grief Observed* after the death of his wife, because it was a diary of pain, bewilderment and emptiness out of keeping with the confident tone of his famous books expounding Christian faith. His was now a grief not discussed but felt like a knife turning in the heart, and his was now a faith not proclaimed from security but tested: 'Where is God? . . . A door slammed in your face . . . After that, silence . . . Supposing the truth were, "God always vivisects"?' Emotions were raw, confused and temporary before peace came.

In a widely ranging study of *The Meanings of Death* (1991) a British theologian, John Bowker, wrote: 'The religious exploration of death is, basically, an assertion of the value of human life and relationships which does not deny, and is not denied by, the absolute fact and reality of death.' If many of the slogans on the banners put into our hands by religion have become hard to believe, and perhaps sometimes hard to take seriously, it would seem that we need a new exploration.

Note

1 From the poem 'Nineteen Hundred and Nineteen', in *Collected Poems of W. B. Yeats*, ed. Richard Finneran (Macmillan, 1991). Reprinted by permission of A. P. Watt Ltd on behalf of Michael B. Yeats and with the permission of Simon & Schuster, New York.

2

Death's Changing Face

THE FACE OF DEATH often changes. To die in a battle is unlike dying in a bed. To die young is unlike dying old. To die in an American hospital when surgical skills, drugs and technology have done their almost miraculous best to postpone or avoid the event is not the same thing as dying in great pain on the floor of a hut in an Indian village. To be a mourner full of silent scepticism about life after death at a funeral in Germany is different from the experience of participating vigorously in African customs which will hasten a new journey to the realm of the ancestors who are remembered and venerated, loved and feared. To be buried in a cemetery which claims on many memorials that it is a dormitory (indeed, 'cemetery' comes from the Greek for 'sleeping place') established by devoted and grieving families, contrasts with being cremated after a brief, sparsely attended, ritual of farewell which may be as cold as the computer that works the cremator. Much of the response to death will depend on whether or not support comes from a strong community, perhaps around the deathbed and certainly at the funeral. And much will depend on how one understands death spiritually, probably because one belongs (more or less) to a spiritual community. There can also be very different levels of awareness that one is confronting death. It is possible to die or grieve in agony. It is also possible to drift off to death without noticing, as one floats on a calm sea of drugs, as it is possible to drug one's own mind into an ability to ignore death.

Of course death is in fact universal and so is the experience of bereavement for survivors, who for a time feel the loss as the death of something in them. For much of the twentieth century it seemed possible, at least in 'developed' countries, to treat death as a taboo subject: it seemed morbid to think about it and tactless to mention it, although murders in fiction were fun. But death could not be banished, not even from the most comfortable or ambitious of societies: two world wars made sure of that and even in times of peace and prosperity the great pretence about death could be felt to be unrealistic. Before the end of the 1960s in the USA, after a time of many protests against what seemed wrong or merely conventional, including many protests against deaths in the Vietnam War, the mystery of death was taken seriously again – as a perpetual mystery which could never be avoided or ended. Here was an evil against which no protest stood a chance, for here was a problem without a solution. But where protests were futile there might be the wisdom of acceptance. Americans, and later an international readership, gave a big response to successors to the *Ars Moriendi* literature, which had produced instructional manuals about the art of dying during the last two centuries of the Middle Ages. The most influential among these books was *On Death and Dying* by Elisabeth Kübler-Ross (1969).

She reminded many readers that the experiences of dying and grieving are common to humanity and themselves have much in common. There is no compulsory timetable (and critics were to say that she ought to have admitted this more clearly) but stages in the reaction to another's death are often similar to the stages in response to the knowledge that one's own death is not far away. First there is stunned anger about the brutality of this interruption of the routines and joys of life. The temptation is great to blame someone, perhaps the person who caused the accident, perhaps the expert who never warned about the dangers of the lifestyle, perhaps the doctor who did not act in time, perhaps the surgeon who made a human error, perhaps other people who have not been sufficiently supportive, perhaps the government which has not funded 'health care' adequately, perhaps oneself. In more traditional societies one may blame witchcraft or displeased ancestors. Then one can take some action – perhaps weeping aloud or silently, perhaps gathering others to share the bitter experience, perhaps making a will or planning some memorial, however small. Then come glimpses of the peace of acceptance, only to find that all the painful emotions flood back. Only by gradual, and often by slow, steps does one gain – or is one given – the strength to enter either death or everyday life with a calmer mind.

Presumably the processes of dying and grieving have often had something of this character but it also seems reasonable to suppose that such disturbing experiences have been felt more keenly in a period when the conventions surrounding death have changed rapidly, as they have done in Britain during the twentieth century. The customs of non-modern peoples have changed so slowly that modern anthropologists or sociologists visiting them have felt that they have been in touch with the 'primitive' or 'timeless'. In 'civilized' or 'advanced' societies there has been much the same reluctance to change, as we have noted in connection with the continued use of the Bible and the clergy at funerals by a population largely non-churchgoing. But in Britain the pace of change during the twentieth century has been extraordinary and the rapidity of change in religious beliefs is unlikely to have been a mere coincidence.

Changes in Scotland and Wales were more cautious, but in England customs changed with a notable rapidity once the state had claimed a new sphere by beginning its systematic registration of deaths in 1837. The Burial Laws of the 1850s ended a long period when the churchyards and vaults of the Church of England had been given a monopoly of corpses by the law, apart from some private cemeteries largely for 'Nonconformists' begun in the 1820s. Cemeteries open to all were now provided by local government, partly because the population was growing, partly because the unhealthy overcrowding of churchyards in cities and towns had been associated with the epidemics of cholera, and partly because of the improved positions of Catholics and Nonconformists. But little account was taken of the prospect of further population growth: graves in Victorian cemeteries were sold or let on 99-year leases like houses and the practice of erecting permanent tombstones over 'ordinary' individuals' graves continued to be taken as normal in contrast with the medieval and later custom of reusing the earth. From 1880, funeral services conducted by non-Anglican clergy were allowed in Anglican churchyards: such toleration was important in the countryside, but the rural churchyards also filled up.

Cremation was declared to be not illegal in 1884; next year three bodies were cremated, and local governments were encouraged to provide crematoria in 1902. By the end of the 1960s cremations outnumbered burials, and by the 1990s almost three-quarters of all deaths were followed by cremation. The clergy of the Church of England had been reluctant to lose their monopoly of burials and were equally reluctant to bless the practice of cremation until two former Archbishops of Canterbury, Lang and

Temple, were cremated in the 1940s. The Roman Catholic Church was slower to accept a practice which seemed to dishonour the dead; official permission was not given before 1964. The Orthodox Churches, Orthodox Judaism and Islam have been very much more reluctant.

It seems probable that no single cause accounted for this revolution in funerary customs. Many factors may be noticed: the end of the monopoly of the parish churchyard ('God's acre'), the filling up of the new cemeteries which used valuable urban land, the feeling that cremation fitted in better with society's new standards of cleanliness and hygiene, the dislike for the 'fuss' of the graveyard burial, the decline in familiarity with church buildings and the clergy, the decline in belief in a future 'resurrection of the body'. Such a combination of strong factors was, it seems, needed to overcome the general repugnance to cremation as a novelty which went against centuries of honouring the dead by a solemn, and almost always definitely religious, burial.

One result of these changes has been that the clergy have lost control of the physical symbolism in most funerals. Although funerals may still be held in churches at the request of the devout, most people have preferred to use the crematorium. This substitute for a church has no purpose other than the burning of corpses in conditions as dignified as possible, with smoke and smell controlled strictly. Little could be done to make the symbolism significant religiously, in contrast with cremation as practised in India. In the Hindu tradition, fire is seen as a purification and as a sacrifice. When a dead human body is burned it is possible to think that the soul ascends to heaven with the smoke and the skull may be broken to make the exit easier. The ashes of the body are entrusted to a river, preferably the Ganges, which is itself sacred and which flows into the mysterious ocean. Family and friends gather round and the eldest son lights the fire and breaks the skull. Less than a fortnight after the death, mourning is supposed to change into respect for an ancestor who may enter another body, a period of invisible purification or the final bliss. But a crematorium which uses enclosed ovens hidden from the mourners, and which reduces the bones to convenient ashes by the action of a machine which spins like a washing machine, seems secular – even if some of the furnishings resemble those to be found in churches and even if a chaplain is present. Perhaps the chaplain is a ghost from the past?

In recent years anthropologists and sociologists have often discussed the 'rites of passage' which mark births, marriages, deaths and some other crises, and they have reached conclusions which are not surprising to those whose duty has been to preside over these occasions or to attend them frequently. An effective 'rite' is a drama of separation from the old status, of transition into a status which is more mysterious or sacred, and of incorporation into a situation which is new both for the person most concerned and for those who are connected. It is like passing through a great doorway. Such rites have been of central importance to countless families and communities in the past, but by these standards many funerals in crematoria have been unimpressive. Most of the mourners have been shielded from the 'absolute fact and reality of death' because they have never seen the dead body; there is little that is mysterious or sacred in the factory-like crematorium; and because there are few beliefs about death which are held with conviction both by the society at large and in the individual's mind and heart, there is no strong drama proclaiming entry into a new stage of life. And this emotional inadequacy of the crematorium comes at the end of a process of dying which has not been supported by the customs of the past – customs which normally had their centre in the home.

In Britain the home had ceased to be the scene of most deaths by the end of the 1950s. Just over half of all deaths now occur in hospitals, eighteen per cent in residential homes for the elderly and four per cent in the hospices which have recently set new standards in the care of the dying. Fewer people gather round a deathbed: the centuries are over when most people lived in small villages, in stable families and in societies which took a great interest in the behaviour of a dying person during what was usually a short crisis. In the Middle Ages the accepted custom was that strangers who saw a priest carrying the 'last sacraments' to a deathbed joined the little procession to the home and were welcome to witness the brief service before withdrawing, but now curtains are drawn when death takes place in a hospital ward. In many traditional societies there have been rules of conduct when on a deathbed, with many equivalents to the 'art of dying' familiar to the Middle Ages. It is hoped that the chief actor in this scripted drama will give an accurate, memorable and edifying performance. Now, however, the dying are almost always left either to doze under the influence of drugs which make them feel 'comfortable' or to invent their own uncomfortable responses to challenges of pain and distress never previously experienced. How to behave when in the valley of the shadow of death is not the only challenge: there is also the problem of how to respond to visitors. Not knowing what it is appropriate to say or do, visitors may try to reduce the awkwardness of the visit by congratulating the patient on looking so well, discussing when he or she will leave the hospital (alive), and being deeply concerned about the weather. There is a great contrast with the Hindu custom of placing a light beside the person dying to guide the soul into the future.

In a modern death scene, hope turns to the professional 'health carers' who naturally and properly concentrate on the exercise of their trained skills. The expertise can include the giving of emotional support, but inevitably what is chiefly required is the ability to prevent, postpone or reverse death. Resuscitations are often possible even when breathing has stopped and the heart no longer beats. One comparatively minor consequence of this medical and surgical miracle-working is that neither the patient nor the visitors can guess as accurately as in the past when death will occur. What is clear is that the physician or surgeon has replaced the priest as the expert most in demand and 'the hour of our death' appears not to be decided by the Almighty. In Britain ethnic minorities often find it difficult to adjust their customs to those of the hospital; for example, it is important for Hindus and Sikhs that they should die on the ground or, if need be, on the floor, as a gesture of humble acceptance. And the novelty of modern practices is such that in Britain there has arisen a movement to bring back 'natural death' in the home, although it is still the wish to have death without pain.

The treatment of the body immediately after death is now left to the professionals, whose businesses have greatly expanded since the pioneers 'undertook' to take care of the bodies and funerals of a few of the rich (in Britain around 1680). No longer is the care of the body the last responsibility towards this person of the women of the family or of the neighbour who was given a small payment to 'lay out'. Death must be dealt with by the experts – but about what it means, no one is an expert. Society itself, which over most of history has laid down the law even in the presence of death, now says 'don't know'.

This summary of the reality in Britain at the close of the twentieth century AD is, however, not intended to suggest that all the customs of earlier ages were better. No one wishes to revive the medical ignorance which in the Middle Ages led to Death being pictured as a skeleton striking suddenly and at random. No one wishes to return to the standard of hygiene which led to the reduction of the European population by about one-third as the Black Death was spread in the fourteenth century. No one wishes the young to die in the numbers which over many centuries meant that parents could be afraid to grow too fond of them. No one wishes to bring back the deathbed agonies which were frequent until the use of opium as a relief began in the eighteenth century. And the picture given by some historians of deathbeds in the old days being surrounded by clergy, families and neighbours has been criticized by other scholars as romantic: the poor often died as they had lived, unhonoured.

No one wishes to restore the oppressiveness of many traditional customs of mourning, when some had to accept intrusions into their heartbreak while others had to demonstrate a grief they did not feel; when the rich felt obliged to display their status even after this blow from the Great Leveller while the poor had to spend money which was needed by the living. The history of funerals in modern France is instructive: the monopoly of the Catholic clergy was so resented that the Revolution attempted to end all traditional marks of respect for the dead. Napoleon shrewdly restored funerals but regulated their expense; then in 1881 an anti-clerical government stopped the division of cemeteries into areas for rich and poor and for Catholics, Protestants and unbelievers.

No one now could applaud the frequency with which the 'wake' after a funeral was regarded as an excuse for a party which might degenerate into drunken horseplay. No one could admire the customs which, when the men had staggered home from the wake, kept widows in black for the rest of their lives (or at least for a long time of depression) and discouraged second marriages. Under these rigid conventions it was not necessary to persuade or force a widow to join her husband on the funeral pyre (as in the Indian practice of *sutee*, outlawed in 1829), for the fate of the widow who 'survived' was in the category now called 'social death'. Merry widows existed, but were talked about because they were both rare and under suspicion.

Moreover, the traditional burial could be as distressing as the modern cremation, for no easy option can follow the end of the body's life. It had been taught, and may have been believed, that bodies would be raised from their graves on the Last Day but the immediate prospect was known to be an utterly humiliating putrefaction. Whether or not it was thought to be polluting to touch a corpse (some superstitions claimed that it brought good luck), there could be disgust at the foul smells and fear of the real danger of infection. There could be defensive jokes about the hungry worms, but also seriously depressed thoughts about the fate of all human pride, when Shakespeare's 'golden lads and girls' all 'come to dust'.

For better or worse, such have been some of the changes in Britain in the past half-century. But elsewhere in the English-speaking world, death has not changed so drastically.

In the USA, as in Britain, most deaths now occur in hospitals or 'rest homes' but other relevant customs are usually different. At present cremation is chosen by less than a quarter of the population. The practice is likely to grow, partly because the cemeteries which occupy about two million acres are filling up, but if so there is likely to be much resistance or regret. American customs before burial are intended to remove or conceal much of the unpleasantness. The practice of embalming (by extracting some fluids and injecting others) became widespread after its use to soften the tragedies of the Civil War in the 1860s, when the bodies of many young soldiers had to be taken home, as was the body of the murdered President Lincoln. The effects do not last for more than a few weeks but the purpose of the skill of the mortician is to prepare for an acceptable 'memory picture' when the body is viewed by mourners, usually in the chapel of the funeral parlour or 'home'. Cosmetics are also used on the face as the deceased rests in a casket which can be padded and laid among many flowers. After the funeral, which is often held in the same chapel, a slow procession of automobiles, respected by other traffic, moves to the burial which also usually has a definitely religious character. The casket is often buried in a concrete or metal grave which separates it from the earth. The monuments may express strong sentiments of love and hope in a cemetery which may be landscaped as a park. All over the USA there are now cemeteries modelled on the pioneers, Grove Street Cemetery in New Haven (1796) and Mount Auburn Cemetery in Boston (1831). In another striking contrast with British customs, cemeteries are usually in private ownership and the competition between the owners is a factor in maintaining high standards of upkeep. It is an accepted practice for a funeral director to own a cemetery. From embalming to burial, the care of the dead is an industry which most Americans are content to see making profits because they want what it offers, the 'last great necessity'.

These practices were mocked by two English writers who felt superior to them – Evelyn Waugh (in *The Loved One*, 1948) and Jessica Mitford (in *The American Way of Death*, 1963) – and there have been a few American protests. Criticism can allege commercialism ('funeral directors' are said to get rich by exploiting a family's grief) and sentimentality (the beautification of the dead is said to deny the reality of death and so hinder grief from taking its natural course). However, these criticisms have not persuaded most Americans to change their habits. On the contrary, these customs are defended as expressions of the natural and praiseworthy desires to honour the dead and comfort the mourners. Of course death has not been tamed, in the USA or anywhere else, but like the Ancient Egyptians modern Americans have certainly thought it sensible to put effort and expenditure into their response. They have also bought large numbers of books about how to die and how to grieve. It appears that, if so disposed, they would be entitled to write books mocking the heartless post-1950 British customs.

But we should not exaggerate the importance of differences between societies in their customs after deaths. Although the customs of different peoples differ greatly, they are accepted locally because in the crisis of bereavement people are anxious to do what others do: being conventional is itself a source of comfort at a time which may be the shattering of a personal world. However, the funerary customs which are accepted amid this distress may well have different effects on different mourners in dramatizing the reality of death or in camouflaging it, in suggesting this or that belief about life or extinction after death, and in helping or hindering a healthy outcome of the process of grieving. Any generalization will be more or less misleading. In Ancient Egypt twenty million tons of stone could be piled up at colossal expense by a considerable part of the country's manhood to make a pyramid for a pharaoh in accordance with sacred beliefs about life after death, but tomb robbers could break in and remove costly objects thought essential to the dead pharaoh's comfort and even survival, and it seems likely that these cynical thieves included some of the labourers who had just built the pyramid and so knew the secrets of its elaborate security system. If so, these men were not the last people to preserve their personal worlds intact while others were shattered.

More important than any custom connected with the deathbed or with the disposal of the dead body is the question of the meaning of death itself, and responses to that question seem to be influenced by such customs rather than totally decided by them. The absence of formal prayers from the average British deathbed has not necessarily meant the absence of any belief that something survives death, any more than the presence of formal prayers in the average funeral has meant the presence of a strongly held traditional faith. The preference of the French for traditional burial rather than modern cremation does not necessarily mean that they share the liking for churches which is common in the USA: on the contrary, France is at least as secular as Britain. In Sweden the same thoroughly Christian service is used for cremations as for burials, yet Sweden has a much lower level of churchgoing by living adults than does the USA, France or Britain, and this particular survival of tradition appears to owe something to the fact that the Church of Sweden owns most of the crematoria.

In the ancient world, both cremation and burial were practised; in the early centuries the customs were different on the different hills on which Rome was built, we are told, and in the recorded history of Rome burial was replaced by cremation as the fashion and, in its turn, cremation was replaced by burial. The differences between customs appear to have had no decisive effects on beliefs about the condition of the dead. Cremation may be interpreted as helping the soul to escape from the body, or as forcing it to go away, or as getting rid of useless junk, but from all three interpretations there can still arise the belief that something survives while the body burns. Burial may be interpreted as helping the dead to sleep, or as hiding an object which has no further dignity, but in either case it can be believed that the soul lives while the corpse rots. The bones may be left in the grave, or disinterred after a period in order to be kept or reburied in some other place; but in either case there can be a belief that although the flesh is no more, there is life after death. In Bombay, the traditional Parsees dispose of their dead by leaving the bodies to be the food of birds of prey on 'towers of silence' because they do not want either fire or earth to be polluted, but they assure enquirers that they believe that the vultures help the *karp* or spiritual body to escape from the physical body which is being eaten.

In their study of *Celebrations of Death* among non-modern peoples (revised, 1991) Richard Huntington and Peter Metcalf observed that

> corpses are burned or buried, with or without human or animal sacrifice; they are preserved by smoking, embalming or pickling; they are eaten – raw, cooked or rotten; they are ritually exposed as carrion or simply abandoned; or they are dismembered and treated in a variety of these ways. Funerals are the occasion for avoiding people, for fighting or having sexual orgies, for weeping or laughing, in a thousand different combinations.

Many peoples feel that the cannibalism just mentioned is deeply appalling; others accept it as a respectable way of honouring the dead because it absorbs their admired 'life force'. Many peoples are disgusted by reports of merriment or orgies at funerals; to others these seem to be proper ways of restoring the 'life force' after the damage inflicted by death. Some peoples are shocked if mourners are hired, others if undertakers are paid for services which families ought to render. Some disapprove of extravagant funerals, others of extravagant memorials. Some think suicide is sinful, even criminal; others may admire it as heroic. Some think it morbid to dwell on the past, others that it is dangerous to forget ancestors. Some fear corpses; others keep bones or ashes, or even embalmed flesh, in their homes. Also, many non-modern peoples think that death is a process even larger than the time which may be taken in a modern hospital to resuscitate someone or to keep a person alive by artificial means: it may be thought that death is not complete until the flesh has fallen off the bones. Other peoples are much more hasty in pronouncing someone dead, with the result that 'corpses' can sometimes show signs of life.

Obviously these different practices do influence beliefs about the dead; the eminent sociologist Durkheim pointed to a human reality by his observation that some people 'mourn because they weep' and it can be believed that a proper burial or cremation – whatever 'proper' may mean – improves the prospects of the dead.

But one does not have to be a great sceptic to think that everything done to a body after a death matters more to the living than to the dead and may matter to different living people in different ways. Introducing essays on *Death and Representation* (1993), the book's editors summed up the learned discussion: 'Death is necessarily constructed by a culture; it grounds the many ways a culture stabilizes and represents itself, and yet it always does so as a signifier with an incessantly receding, ungraspable signified, always pointing to other signifiers, other means of representing what finally is just absent.' And they put the conclusion even more briefly: 'every representation of death is a misrepresentation'.

It is therefore possible for contrasting representations of death to be held together within the same society and even within the heart and mind of the same individual, for conflicting emotions arise naturally and it is easy to feel that they could never be reconciled or simplified in logic, precisely because the emotions are about 'what finally is just absent'. In Japan, for example, many of the same people attend the temples of what an outsider may regard as rival religions, Buddhism and Shinto. As Maurice Bloch has observed (1992), 'immediately after death the invisible soul of the dead person is believed to be unwilling to leave the house and the community of the living and so it must be cajoled, forced or even tricked into going'. Since this is a widely held belief, 'for ordinary people Buddhism is, by and large, a system for the removal of the dead, whether in body or spirit' and Buddhist monks are regarded as useful (rather than auspicious) when the rites which they perform are thought helpful in this connection. But the Shinto priests also have a function in Japanese society, for they perform and teach the veneration of the dead as ancestors, when the dead are firmly dead. In the annual Bon festival, the souls of the dead are briefly allowed to revisit familiar scenes but the festivities in the Shinto tradition start only when this return has been clearly concluded. And many of the Japanese who at times make use of both the Buddhist and the Shinto traditions nurse their own sceptical thoughts about the possibility of any life after death. Many students of Japanese public opinion have concluded that it is nowadays not a country where belief in God or gods or eternity is held strongly by more than a minority. Perhaps true believers are a quarter of the population.

Whatever is done to the dead body or thought or felt about it, over tens of thousands of years most people have usually believed that life must go on – in one sense for the living (a sense as lively as possible) but also in another for the dead (a sense as good as possible). But in each and every place or time, whatever may be the customs surrounding dying and death, a question is likely to occur to a number of people as they look death in the face: is it true to say that the dead person is somehow alive? This question is the skull which remains beneath death's changing face.

3

Why We Ask

IT IS STILL THE QUESTION which comes with being human – and comes with a particular sharpness when we face without flinching the absolute fact and reality of death. We have grown out of the belief expounded by philosophers in Ancient Greece and Rome that the *aether* is the pure air above the stars and therefore a suitable resting place for the wise and good. (In his *Dream of Scipio* Cicero located there a kind of club where men who had served the state could relax in congenial company.) We have also abandoned the belief, strong in nineteenth-century science, that the 'ether' is an invisible medium in which light travels in waves. With our better science we may know that 'ether' is a colourless liquid made by the action of sulphuric acid on alcohol and useful for deadening the pains of the body. But we still ask: what is the significance of a human death?

Dying continues to be the climax of the often disagreeable process of ageing, although the expectation of years of physical life in 'developed' societies has doubled over the last 200 years. The machine may not be wrecked by some early disaster or disease but it still wears out. Around 250 BC a book was written with an unflinching realism which prevented neither its inclusion in the Hebrew Bible nor its fame under the Greek name *Ecclesiastes*. The sun and moon are clouded over (pleasures grow dimmer by day and night). The arms tremble (possessions cannot be kept secure). Women no longer grind corn (teeth no longer chew). There is no view from the window (eyesight fails). The birds fall silent (hearing goes). The street is full of terrors (walking becomes a worry). These are rehearsals for the hour when the golden bowl (the skull) is broken and the silver cord (the spine) is snapped. *Ecclesiastes* 12 could have added that the identity given by work is lost, loneliness is increased, income is diminished, the bladder causes humiliations, the joints become painful, the heart beats more slowly . . . but these old pictures are still tickets of admission into the grey world of old age.

Dying is often an undignified trauma even if the illnesses with which modern medicine or surgery grapples are chronic or degenerative rather than the diseases which used to be suddenly fatal. Often the decisive event is that the haemoglobin in the blood, made rich in oxygen when pumped by the heart through the lungs, ceases to be life-giving. It cannot carry oxygen to the brain in a sufficient quantity, whether because the heart or a lung ceases to function properly, or because a vital artery is blocked by a clot, or because toxic waste is no longer cleared out. Traditionally, the end of heartbeats and breathing was taken as proof of death, but the emphasis has moved to brain-death as recorded by the EEG machine. With the aid of another machine a 'persistent vegetative state' can be maintained for years when a little activity continues in the brain. But the end comes when no blood reaches the brain over a period of five minutes or less, when no signals can be received or sent by the cortex of the brain and when the cells of the organs and the flesh die gradually. *Rigor mortis* is caused by the contraction of the muscles before they decompose; this is usually the cause of the smiles on the faces of the recently dead.

The cells of the brain cannot be replaced as they die. They do die, one by one, long before the drama of a severe stroke or the slower tragedy of one of the mental illnesses which result from the brain's decay. Other penalties for living, in particular for a long life, may be grouped together under the fearful name of cancer, the process by which cells in the body gradually escape control and divide and proliferate without restraint, wrecking organs and tissues. It is little consolation for the victims to be told how wonderful it is that the cells were reproduced faultlessly for so long.

In the seventeenth century Francis Bacon called death 'the least of all evils'. He admitted that 'groans and convulsions, and a discoloured face, and friends weeping, and blacks, and obsequies and the like, show death terrible', yet he maintained that the human spirit could overcome such distresses: 'there is no passion in the mind of Man so weak, but that it mates and masters the fear of death', with the result that adults need not be like children who 'fear to go into the dark'. He recommended copying the soldier by concentrating on the work of life: 'he that dies in an earnest pursuit is like one that is wounded in hot blood, who for the time scarce feels the hurt'. Therefore the work that needs to be done includes dying with courage; Bacon mentioned stories of Roman emperors dying with lighthearted remarks. He himself died in the pursuit of scientific knowledge, having caught a fatal chill while experimenting with the refrigeration effected by stuffing a chicken with snow. And it is surely true that countless brave women and men (and children) have conquered the fear of death when in danger or when dying, as they have conquered many fears while living: 'mankind's common instinct', William James observed, 'has always held the world to be a theatre for heroism'. But it seems nonsense to call the death the 'least' of all the evils which follow the disturbance of being born.

The Greek philosopher Epicurus, who died around 270 BC, taught that 'death, the most terrifying of ills', ought to be held to be 'nothing to us, since so long as we exist death is not with us and when it comes we do not exist'. He did not intend to recommend the gluttony which has been called 'Epicurean'; to him 'bread and water provide the highest pleasure' and 'if you want to make Pythocles rich do not give him money – diminish his desires'. But in his desire to 'expel the sufferings of the mind' he rolled together into one concept, 'death', four realities which ought to have been considered separately: knowing that we must die, dying, being dead, and knowing that another has died.

He was of course wise to say that the dead cannot experience the pains which are a part of life as we know it but he was not so wise as the poet Sappho, who observed that death cannot be good, else the gods would choose to die. He did not entirely reckon with the fact that before death none of us does enough or learns enough; for example, his own semi-scientific understanding of the human body was so limited that he went to his death believing that the *psyche*, the breath which animates the body, is a kind of gas, a collection of atoms like everything else but one so thin that when the body dies the *psyche* escapes, only to be dispersed in the air. He was also wrong about the process of dying being 'nothing to us'. (It seems likely that even the bravest of us will want to concentrate on dying as we die.) Nor did he come to terms with the disadvantages in being dead. The tradition is that he wrote some 300 books but his influence has been limited because only some short writings and fragments have survived. It is said that his chief pleasure, when not writing, was to talk in his garden with his friends. Surely the prospect of their parting was not 'nothing' to him while he was alive, as grief was certainly not 'nothing' to them when he was dead.

The Roman poet Lucretius put the philosophy of Epicurus into stately words which have influenced many of those able to read his language. He too saw atoms everywhere, he too argued that 'the man who does not exist cannot be miserable' and he too hoped that people would no longer make a hell for themselves on earth by believing the myths about suffering on the other side of death. We know that some Romans shared his scepticism; the poet Catullus memorably believed that 'suns may rise again but ours is an eternal sleep'. Some surviving tombs carry the inscription 'I was not, I was, I am not, I do not care': it was so easily recognizable that sometimes only the first letters of the Latin words were carved. Yet the people who caused such a tomb to be made must have cared about this particular death, and the person being commemorated must have thought enough about the end to wish for the carving of the words which defied the conventional beliefs.

Many more tombs were inscribed with conventional words such as 'May the earth lie lightly on you!' Roses and other flowers were placed on the graves, lead pipes sometimes connected food with the coffin, and twice a year in Rome festivals were held which were thought to recall the dead literally. Roman law decreed that graves and burial vaults must never be violated: that was why the catacombs used by the hated Christians were left undisturbed. Rome's greatest poet, Virgil, felt obliged to conduct a tour of the world inhabited by the dead. In *Death and Burial in the Roman World* (1971) J. M. C. Toynbee concluded that 'among the great majority of people in the Roman age . . . there persisted and prevailed a conviction that some kind of conscious existence is in store for the soul after death and that the dead and the living can affect one another mutually'.

In philosophy the Stoic movement was like the Epicurean in that it attempted to make people invulnerable to the disturbances of life and death, and thus to make them content to sing 'the song of life'. But the Stoics knew that it was unrealistic to pursue the aim of Epicurus to be completely aloof from all troubles. Thus the philosopher Seneca took the risk of becoming involved in the politics of the Roman empire at the very top. He became the tutor of the young Nero and for a time that emperor's chief adviser. He urged people to overcome the fear of death not by trying to ignore it but by thinking about it. On occasion he could make good use of the Stoic teaching that the soul is a 'spark' of the universe, which is itself a 'spark' of God. A letter survives which consoled a mother who had lost a son. The soul, Seneca wrote, consists of *aether* and returns at death to where it came from, above the stars. Elsewhere he admitted that he, too, was uncertain: if anything remains of us after our deaths it must be 'the better part', even 'God in a human body' (and therefore stories about punishments in hell are mere fables), but our survival may be a 'charming dream'. Whether consoling grief or confessing to ignorance, however, he was consistent in rejecting the 'I do not care' attitude to death. He could not be aloof when ordered to commit suicide by the emperor, formerly his pupil. A later and better emperor who was also a Stoic philosopher, Marcus Aurelius, left behind *Meditations* full of the sense that since immortality is a dream, the pleasures of life are stupid.

'There is no death', someone exclaims in a play by André Malraux. 'There is only *me*, *me*, who is going to die.' In Tolstoy's most moving short story, Ivan Ilych accepts in the abstract that there is death, but he feels it for the first time when he meets it: after a lifetime of limited success as a lawyer and in his family, he is going to be put through the agony and disgusting squalor of death by cancer. Only at the end does he accept his own mortality. In existentialist philosophy it is constantly stressed that the death towards which I move every day, or grief for the death of another who was dear in past days, is what makes me ask what I really am, what my existence means, what another's life meant. Martin Heidegger's philosophy is not the most accessible intellectual achievement of the twentieth century, but at least he can be understood by many when he teaches that the vision of 'being-there' (*Dasein*) as 'being-towards-death' is what encourages the authentically personal expression of one's essential identity. One escapes from the passive acceptance of other people's ideas (the 'They-self') and from the stupidity of worldliness through this sense of an ending, this 'freedom-towards-death'. 'Once one has grasped that one's existence must end, one is snatched back from the endlessly many possibilities which offer themselves as being closest: being comfortable, being detached, being careless . . . ' So death provides the highest education. The 'possibility of the impossibility of any existence at all' opens to us not only the wonder that we die but also the wonder that we exist. It awakens in us Kierkegaard's questioning: 'Where am I? Who am I? What is this thing called the world? How did I come into the world? Why was I not consulted? . . . And if I am compelled to take part in it, where is the manager? I should like to see him.' Kierkegaard, who was more easily intelligible than Heidegger because he told stories, maintained that without the prospect of death, life itself would be tasteless, and he used a story about a tombstone in England commemorating 'the Unhappiest Man'. When opened the grave contained no corpse.

But the result of this awakening may be despair. In the nineteenth century, Kierkegaard the 'gloomy Dane' was more or less a lone voice, but in the twentieth century, other writers communicated existentialism by stories as well as by philosophy, and they found many readers who understood them in that age of anxiety lived under the shadows cast by the two world wars and the nuclear threats. Contradicting Heidegger, Jean-Paul Sartre presented the chanciness, finality and universality of death as proof that human life is itself ultimately meaningless: 'we are absurd when we live and absurd when we die'. 'If we die our life has no sense,' he concluded, 'because our problems do not receive any kind of solution and their own meaning remains undetermined.' For a time he saw some meaning in resistance to the Nazis and in Communism, but he died disillusioned. Albert Camus, who met his own death in a car crash, found a more permanent meaning by understanding life as a long rebellion against death – a doomed rebellion, of course. Many other existentialist quotations about death could be assembled but *angst* (dread) as a mood of many of the sensitive in much of the twentieth century does not need to be shown to be a fact – and, anyway, no expression of a feeling which has surfaced in many generations has been more eloquent, or better known, than

> All our yesterdays have lighted fools
> The way to dusty death. Out, out, brief candle!
> Life's but a walking shadow, a poor player
> That struts and frets his hour upon the stage
> And then is heard no more; it is a tale
> Told by an idiot, full of sound and fury,
> Signifying nothing.

Shakespeare put these words into the mouth of Macbeth, a bereaved murderer, not long after the death of his own brother, a young actor. Yet the human quest for meaning even in death has never stopped. Animals often fear death when it seems to be imminent: that is why they escape from predators as rapidly as possible. But only the human animal seems to be acutely aware, with fear and trembling, that death is inescapable although it may still be distant, and only the human animal seems to be indignant long before it happens that this will be the end and that no one knows what, if anything, will follow it. Pascal said:

> When I consider the short duration of my life, swallowed up in eternity past and to come, the little space that I fill or can see, engulfed in the infinite immensity of spaces of which I am ignorant and which know me not, I am terrified and astonished . . . We run towards the precipice having put something before our eyes so that we do not see it.

And what would we see if we could look? About 4,000 years ago, in Ancient Egypt, *The Song of the Harper* lamented:

> No one comes back from that place,
> To tell us how they live,
> To tell us what they need,
> To quieten our hearts until we go there.

In his first letter to Corinth, St Paul called death 'the last enemy' (15:26). Like much other deep thinking about death, his insights were expressed with the aid of mythology – in his case, with the aid of the myth that Adam and Eve forfeited access to the Tree of Life, the fruit of which would have enabled them to live for ever. But a myth can refer to a reality which may perhaps be indicated in less picturesque words. Most eloquently in the first third of his letter to the Christians in Rome, Paul conveyed his vision of death as the inevitable penalty for living 'in accordance with the flesh' or (as in another translation) 'on the level of mere human nature'. He saw that death rules over human life and rules by fear. It creates despair even before it strikes, for it is expected, and unavoidably it comes, as the climax of everything that decays into corruption. All our disappointments, and all our failures, are little rehearsals for the end –

but this final, total negation, the terror of being sentenced to death, is the most effective of the innumerable messages which tell us that we have fallen very far short of the glory towards which we once aspired. With his fellow Pharisees, Paul had himself struggled heroically to obey the Law of Moses with its instructions for the truly good life, but along with the whole of humankind he had found himself imprisoned in the moral and physical squalor of the 'law of sin and death'. So he cried: 'Wretched creature that I am, who will rescue me from this body of death?' (Romans 7:24).

A prominent theme in the ancient myths of Mesopotamia was the importance of accepting the frontier between the living and the 'land of no return'. That must be asserted against any feelings of grief or curiosity. The gods themselves could be killed but only they could successfully return from the land of the dead, as Tammuz did each spring. This world and all its inhabitants were believed to have been created out of the remains of a supernatural being who died and remained dead.

Gilgamesh was the king of Uruk about 5,000 years ago, and clay tablets which seem to have been made about 1,000 years later record stories about his adventures with his friend Enkidu and his inconsolable grief when that hero died. It was not enough for him to feed the spirit of his friend with loaves of bread and jars of beer left on the grave, as was the custom. A mixture of parents – human and divine – had left some divine blood in him, so he thought he could do more. Determined to secure immortality for Enkidu and himself, he explores the underworld (which began just beneath the graves) and he has many further adventures as he passes through great mountains, the 'land of the scorpion people' and a country of thick darkness, plus a temptation by the 'wine maiden', before finally reaching the abode of the dead. There he makes his request and is given the test of being able to keep awake for seven nights. He fails and is taunted: 'The hero who seeks life cannot resist sleep!' He is given a further chance: he must find a plant which grows at the bottom of the sea, for to eat it is to gain eternal youth. After further adventures he does find it but before he eats he goes swimming, only to find that a snake has stolen the plant.

A later myth told of a queen, Innana or Ishtar, who also penetrated into the underworld. She could not take courtiers with her, although royal tombs which have been excavated contained the bones of many slaughtered servants. Instead she found that seven walls guarded the city of the dead and at each gateway she was stripped of more and more of her jewels and clothes. When she reached the palace of the queen of the dead she was killed. She was revived and even allowed to return to the land of the living, but she had to send a substitute to take her place among the dead. Gilgamesh voices the obvious conclusion to the thoughts behind such myths: 'Shall I not die just like Enkidu?' Thus in the Mesopotamia of the ancient Sumerians and Babylonians death is 'the battle which none can win' – and which none can understand, for 'you cannot see death any more than you can look at the sun'.

The same theme is to be found in some other ancient myths. One from Japan, almost identical with the Greek story of Orpheus and Euridice, tells of a hero, Izanagi, who went to seek his wife in the land of the dead. In recognition of his love and courage he is promised that he can bring her back to the world of the living if he shows that he trusts the promise by not looking back while he is leading her out of the darkness. When near the exit he does look back, only to see that she is a decaying corpse. In terror he rushes into the daylight, alone.

A comprehensive acceptance of death is reflected in a myth told in pre-Christian Scandinavia and Germany. Although what may follow the deaths of ordinary people is not so attractive (*Hel* was originally a goddess but became a world), heroes could undertake further adventures after dying glorious deaths in battle, and could drink and fight in Valhalla, the 'Hall of the Slain'. Eventually, however, even the heroes with the loudest bravado, and even the gods, would all be killed in the Great Winter and in the battle of Ragnarok. The forces of chaos would prevail and even the sun would be swallowed up. There could be a glimpse of a new world inhabited by the sons of the gods, but it was never more than a glimpse.

People have sometimes wondered whether this all-embracing fate of death could have been avoided. It may have seemed sensible to ask this question in the long ages when people usually died young and when the most frequent causes were infectious diseases which struck suddenly and fatally, or the violence of nature, of animals or of enemies, or simple accidents. So death could be blamed on devils, on witches or on angry ancestors. And it could be blamed on the foolish arrogance of the first humans or on sheer bad luck.

The myth of Adam (meaning 'Man') and Eve ('Life') in the form preserved in the Bible (in Genesis 3) seems to date from about

950 BC, when the Israelites had acquired a sophistication also reflected in their stories about their two most memorable kings, David and Solomon. The story incorporates much folk wisdom: human bodies are not entirely different from the earth; men are stronger than women (they once had a spare rib); women have to put up with their husbands, with the pain of childbirth and with much else because they need men and children; people are sexy (fruit is 'pleasing to the eye and tempting') yet also ashamed to be seen naked; men have to survive by the sweat of their brows; snakes seem to be immortal because they shed their skins yet crawl on the ground and are dangerous. But at the heart of the story, planted at the centre of the garden of Eden ('Bliss'), stands the Tree of Life.

This tree bears fruit which, if eaten, would enable Adam and Eve to live for ever. But the fruit is never eaten, for an angel with a 'whirling and flashing sword' is always on duty to prevent access. This is not because the humans have bad luck: it is because they are too proud already, having eaten from the Tree of Knowledge. The 'knowledge' they have acquired may be merely the skill to distinguish between what is useful and what is not, but it is usually understood to include the ability to decide what is good and what is evil. So the arrogance of Adam and Eve is their downfall. Yet the God who had breathed into Adam's nostrils the breath of life does not become an enemy; he does not carry out the threat he has issued of capital punishment 'on the day' should the embargo on the Tree of Knowledge be broken. On the contrary, God becomes a tailor, making 'tunics of skins' to cover the couple's nudity, and Adam is allowed to live for 930 years. The Creator's basic intention is that humankind shall live for ever, but people are arrogant, people refuse to live according to God's plan, and so people are humbled by all having to die one day. Such is the answer conveyed by this myth to the question which an alarmed Adam heard when God was walking in the garden and enjoying the cool of the evening breeze: 'Where are you?'

It could also be thought, less profoundly, that death might have been avoided, had humanity not been cursed from the beginning with rotten luck. Many stories have been told of how two messengers were sent by the gods to the first humans. One (sometimes the chameleon) carried the promise of immortality, the other (sometimes the lizard) brought the prospect of death. The more welcome messenger was delayed by some accident or diversion. That seemed to be typical of the misfortunes of life – and the first death cut the humans off from any share in the power and understanding of the gods, as the ladder linking heaven and earth was broken or the Celestial Mountain lost its top.

Sometimes it has been believed that by their skills including magic, or by the quality of their lives including morality, some people can live for ever although they die. The largest industry in Ancient Egypt was the manufacture of tombs and coffins, with their contents, in order that the souls of the dead, or at any rate of the royal and the rich among the dead, might enjoy everlasting life. Among the writings on the walls of the pyramids or rock-tombs, or on the sides of coffins, or on papyrus placed inside the coffins, were texts to be used by the dead in order to show the gods that they were entitled to this life. It would be a good life, worth all the trouble and the investment: a pharaoh could now expect to join the sun-god in his daily journey around the flat earth (in a boat supplied for that exalted purpose) while a farmer could expect to grow abundant crops, and to enjoy hunting, in the Fields of Reeds which were remarkably like the valley of the Nile at its best. These texts were magical, giving guidance about how to avoid the many dangers to be met in the course of the journey to be judged by the gods. Even during this judgement, magic might do the trick. A text from about 1400 BC supplies a formula to be recited which will 'purge the dead from all the evil he has done': it confesses to no sin but is a boastful catalogue of good deeds. That is scarcely the summit in the history of ethics, but it does suggest that the attention of the god called the Eater of the Dead, and condemnation to a hell where it would have been a mercy to be eaten, could be avoided by a parade of human goodness.

Although a prayer to the heart not to 'bear witness' against the claim to goodness could be included among the magic spells, there could also be a sense that morality had to be genuine in order to pass muster. The heart had to be weighed against a feather taken from the splendid hat worn by Maat the goddess of truth and justice. An instruction left by a pharaoh for his son around 2100 BC warns that 'a man remains after his death and his deeds are placed before him in heaps'. Moreover, the president of the court which judged the dead knew the difference between right and wrong. He was Osiris, murdered by his brother Seth, resurrected by his wife Isis and avenged by his son Horus. A dead pharaoh became Osiris in some sense, meaning that his successor had to become Horus: the system of truth and justice, itself called Maat, had to be maintained. Thus the myths of Ancient Egypt were more moral than the myths of Ancient Mesopotamia. There, no distinction between the good and the bad was made in the land of no return. All the dead were only half-alive and the least uncomfortable in this underworld were not the righteous but those fortunate enough to have fathered many sons who could supply the food and drink from the surface of the earth. For the Egyptians, people were graded in death as in life.

On the whole, however, the myths of non-modern peoples accept the prospect that everyone will die. An Indonesian story is that the gods let down from heaven two objects in response to the prayers of the first humans: a stone and a banana. The human choice of the banana suggests that since people need food, and no animal, tree, or plant which provides food lives for ever, they cannot expect to last for as long as the rocks.

Indeed, some of the myths see advantages in one generation following another in the rhythm of life. One story of the South Pacific imagines a time when people could become immortal if they so chose. A mother entered magic water and emerged young; but her child did not recognize her and after that rejection she chose to be natural and therefore to be old.

Another myth, found in Madagascar, tells how the first humans were told by the gods that they could be deathless but must choose between the immortality of the moon, which waxes and wanes but always recovers itself, and the immortality of the tree, which dies – but not before it produces seeds which continue to live. The first humans, wanting children, chose to be like the tree.

More recent wrestling with the mystery of death has had much in common with the ancient encounters with the unchanging end.

Many people are like the first humans in that myth, feeling that despite its initial attractions an immortality of sheer continuity, going on experiencing, doing and thinking the same things for ever and ever, would become so boring as to be intolerable. William Blake praised the wise mortal who 'kisseth the joy as it flies' and the meaning of this is easily understandable: we enjoy most intensely pleasures which we know will not last for ever, much as we enjoy a hot drink which is going to get cold. If we enjoy our work also, it is in response to the challenge to get a job done within a given time, and certainly in a lifetime, for even the person most absorbed in work would not be so absorbed if there was no clock ticking in the background. All this is obviously true about human life, its joys and its jobs. So, with the prospect of Andrew Marvell's 'deserts of vast eternity' as our future, *carpe diem*, seize the day! Yet it is also true that when such strict limits are set to any human pleasure or achievement the sense of finitude can be a bottomless source of anxiety or sadness. Blake advocated kissing the fleeting joy – but in his equally ardent advocacy of embracing a permanent joy, he struggled to share a vision which would enable the frustrated to live 'in eternity's sunrise'. He was extremely frustrated in his own work and passionately believed in immortality. When his brother died he thought he saw the soul rise into the air, clapping.

It need not be thought that the attainment of an endless day of joy is the supreme reason for clapping when death ends our darkness. It can be maintained that humanity's struggle is best directed not towards happiness, fleeting or permanent, but towards the less selfish goals: the discovery of truth, the contemplation of beauty, the growth of the goodness which is outgoing love. Therefore, over the centuries it has often been argued, by teachers who do not deserve to be despised, that if these intellectual and moral efforts are to be fulfilled and rewarded, the end of a lifetime's attempts must be immortality. And it has even been argued that when we exercise gifts in the realms of truth, beauty and goodness we are doing something which is itself immortality, because these 'gifts' of ours are literally gifts, given to us by God or gods.

Aristotle, the philosopher who is often honoured as the first true scientist, rejected the views of his teacher Plato about the immortality of the detachable human soul (*psyche*), as he rejected Plato's fondness for myths and his scorn for the study of natural objects. To him the 'soul' was the 'form' of the body: it was the life which animates and organizes a body and, as it feeds and reproduces, makes it live. All animals, birds and reptiles have souls in that sense; so, in a rather different way, do stars, planets, trees, plants and even cabbages. These souls die when their bodies die. What is shared by God with human beings is *nous*, the 'rational' (not the 'sensitive' or 'vegetative') soul. This can survive the body's death, but without consciousness or memory. It is not personal; it cannot be polluted; it does not need to be purified, punished or rewarded. And reason, the divine and immortal power, can guide humans to live according to its instructions. Aristotle wrote that 'we must not follow those who urge us, being human, to reason and choose humanly and, being mortal, in a mortal way, but so far as is possible we must immortalize and spare no effort to live in accordance with the best in us'.

Immanuel Kant, who has a good claim to be regarded as the greatest modern philosopher, argued for our immortality in answer to the question which he held to be among the most important of all questions: 'For what may we hope?'

In *Religion within the Limits of Reason Alone* (1793) he maintained that 'proofs' used to support traditional beliefs about God could all be questioned or contradicted by 'pure' reason. He also insisted that 'we know nothing of the future'. Yet the 'practical' reason needed for the business of living a good life demanded belief in three realities: God, freedom and immortality. God is needed in order to make the world ultimately meaningful; the freedom of the will is needed in order to explain the conviction that we are free to obey the imperatives of our consciences; immortality is needed to fulfil and reward our feeble moral struggles. Kant was a Protestant philosopher who defined and defended the Enlightenment of the eighteenth century but Karl Rahner, one of the leading Roman Catholic philosophical theologians in the twentieth century, also maintained that immortality is needed as the ultimate vindication and completion of the very long story of the human turning to 'transcendence' and the human choice of 'the good'.

In his book on *The Tragic Sense of Life*, written in the early years of the twentieth century, the Spanish sage Miguel de Unamuno bore witness to this vision of a good end, being challenged by the modern ways of reasoning amid the tragedy of the deaths in the First World War. To him the tragedy of all human life was that the drama makes sense only if immortality is true – but that outcome cannot be known for sure.

> We must needs believe in the other life, in the eternal life beyond the grave, and in an individual and personal life, in a life in which each one of us may feel his consciousness and feel that it is united, without being confounded, with all other consciousnesses in the Supreme Consciousness, in God; we must needs believe in that other life in order that we may live in this life, and endure it, and give it meaning and finality. And we must needs believe in that other life, perhaps, in order that we may deserve it, in order that

> we may obtain it, for it may be that a person neither deserves it nor will obtain it who does not passionately desire it above reason and, if need be, against reason.

It was not what either Aristotle or Kant would have written, but de Unamuno's heart had its reasons.

If our own power of reasoning seems to contradict any belief in a power greater than ourselves supporting human aspirations, some consolation may be found in the thought that others carry on when we are gone.

If one lives to a ripe old age and to the experience of failing powers, it is not unusual to feel that the fruit is ready to drop off the tree into the dust. The natural end can even be welcomed in our weariness, as recommended in Edmund Spenser's *Fairie Queene*:

> Sleep after toil, port after stormy seas,
> Ease after war, death after life, doth greatly please.

However, this advice offered by a character called Despaire is not much of a consolation if it is believed that the fruit of a human life is left to rot and that any ship approaching this harbour is wrecked at the port's entrance. Even in the more prosperous countries, until the nineteenth century AD most people died in infancy or youth. The frost blighted the bud on the tree and the storm sank their hopes when the voyage had scarcely begun. And of how many longer lives is it true to say that their 'toil' has been obviously significant? The effect of a lament for the victims of war such as the *War Requiem* of Britten is not only to deepen our sense of the tragedy of young lives ended in battles arranged by older men; it is also to deepen our sense of death as the universal tragedy, a theme which runs through the work of Britten's later years, down to *Death in Venice*.

Certainly one is entitled to some satisfaction if one's impact on the world is such that one can join George Eliot's 'choir invisible'

> Of the immortal dead who live again
> In minds made better by their presence.

George Eliot has certainly joined the immortals in that way. But of how many others is that true? Monuments in churches and public places, tombstones in churchyards and cemeteries, and war memorials cry 'Remember!' But almost always after a few years the names are forgotten. In the twentieth century, Communist governments attempted to answer people's remaining anxieties about death by assuring them that the heroes of the people's struggle would live for ever in the hearts of the people. But before the century ended leading Communists were being remembered only to be denounced. In many earlier centuries Chinese emperors made elaborate arrangements to secure their positions after death, but in the course of time the 6,000 *terracotta* soldiers guarding the body of one emperor have become far more famous than him. Oblivion has also been the fate of many humbler Chinese people who were in their days loved more than any emperor. They could hope that their descendants would guard memories, and for a time this happened: indeed, the reverence shown to tablets inscribed with the names of dead family members could be called by contemptuous Westerners who misunderstood it 'ancestor worship'. But eventually these tablets were hidden away and forgotten, as new generations felt nothing about remote ancestors. If, as many peoples believe, people live after death only for so long as they are remembered, immortality is not secure for most of us.

It is often said that we 'live on' in our children. But since in fact we die and our children go their own ways into their own lives and deaths, the survival is far from complete. We may be missed, but the reality is that we must make room for our successors who have the advantage of youth and energy. Parents ought not to be surprised, for they have had to learn to let go of any illusion that grown children still find them indispensable. We are born into a world where countless things and people have had to die in order that we may live. Stars had to die if our bodies were to contain the heavier elements such as carbon which our own planet could not produce. Hundreds of millions of tiny sperms perished in the effort to push into my mother's egg the one sperm which would make me. Many more species have become extinct than have survived into our own stage of evolution. The dinosaurs who for about 160 million years seemed to be evolution's greatest triumph had to die if the very much smaller animals who were our ancestors were to have a chance to make the future. About 4,000 million years of life on this planet died before *Homo sapiens* evolved between 100,000–200,000 years ago. Multitudes of our human predecessors made great sacrifices, including the laying down of their lives, in order to build civilization. All around us creatures are eaten by other creatures and the same process supplies our own dinners. In some 2,000 million years or so human life will no longer be sustainable on this planet because the processes which have made it possible cannot go on for ever. Within 3,000 million years or so of that death, our planet will be reabsorbed into the sun and at a later date the sun will die . . .

An ancient Hindu myth tells of the anger of the Creator, Brahma, because he is frustrated: he has created so many beings on earth that there is no longer room for them all. He is advised by Shiva, who at that stage of the development of the Hindu tradition was a subordinate god, to arrange that they may die and return to the world through repeated rebirths: in that way the Creator will conserve his energy and everyone will have space. So Brahma creates 'a dark maiden attired in red robes' and he names her Death. At first she refuses to carry out her terrible task. She retires and weeps for millions of years. But in the end Brahma persuades her to do her duty and her tears become the diseases which carry off mortals when their hour has come. I may not agree that Shiva found the answer in reincarnation but I have to admit that Brahma the Creator had a problem. I have to leave the world because, like a hotel, it could not accommodate guests who stay for ever.

But I ask: into what do I disappear? And rightly or wrongly it does not seem to be enough to point to the grave or the crematorium by way of an answer.

Baruch Spinoza was a philosopher who maintained that because the fear of death is one of the passions which cause 'human bondage' the free man 'thinks of death less often than anything else'. A man of noble character, he had freed himself from any selfish hope of personal survival while not entirely abandoning the tradition of Jewish mysticism. He had a religious attitude to 'God or Nature' and believed in the union of 'something imperishable' in the human spirit with the 'unchangeable' source of all that exists for a time. He maintained that 'love towards an eternal and infinite object alone feeds the mind with joy and itself is completely free from all sadness' and in that faith he remained calm as he died, in 1677.

Early in the nineteenth century Shelley expressed essentially the same faith in his lament for Keats:

> Dust to the dust! but the pure spirit shall flow
> Back to the burning fountain whence it came,
> A portion of the Eternal! . . .
> He is made one with Nature, there is heard
> His voice in all her music, from the moan
> Of thunder to the song of the night's sweet bird . . .
> He is a portion of the loveliness
> Which once he made more lovely.

But a great snag about any immortality which 'God or Nature' can provide is that it does not usually seem to leave any room for the survival or resurrection of the individual. (Another snag is that the universe itself does not seem to be immortal.) Keats had thought of this sad world as 'a vale of soul-making' but had died very painfully at the age of 24, believing that his name was 'writ in water'. If he was 'made one with Nature' in the end, had his 'soul' been made in vain? So far as Nature reveals, the existence of Shelley ended when he was drowned in a storm and cremated on a beach: a friend remembered how his brain bubbled in the fire. It seems that before the arrival of Christianity the Celts often believed that at death a soul migrates not into heaven or a new human body but into a particular natural object such as a tree, but unless this is believed Nature offers no final refuge to the individual. Richard Dawkins is one of the twentieth-century scientists who have ended their studies of the treatment of individuals by Nature with atheism. He communicated his gloom-and-doom vision in *River Out of Eden* (1996):

> The total amount of suffering per year in the natural world is beyond all decent computation . . . If there is ever a time of plenty, this very fact will automatically lead to an increase in population until the natural state of starvation and misery is restored . . . The universe we observe has precisely the properties we should expect if there is, at bottom, no design, no purpose, no evil and no good, nothing but blind, pitiless indifference.

Many people who use their eyes and brains find something more encouraging than that in what they see, but it can never be easy to combine honesty with unstinted praise for Mother Nature as a model of unfailing tenderness to each one of us. Writing his

History of the World and awaiting his own execution, Sir Walter Ralegh saw this. 'O eloquent, just and mighty Death! . . . thou hast drawn together all the far-fetched greatness, all the pride, cruelty and ambition of Man, and covered it all over with these two narrow words: Hic jacet!' (Here lies . . .)

So was the Welsh poet Dylan Thomas being totally realistic when he urged his dying father to 'rage, rage against the dying of the light'? Or did the Indian poet Tagore see a more important part of reality when he said that 'death is not extinguishing the light: it is putting out the lamp because the dawn has come'? *Homo sapiens* differs biologically from the chimpanzee, we are told, by no more than 1.6 per cent of the chromosomes, the carriers of heredity's instructions to the body. Does such a tiny difference justify our applauding Sir Thomas Browne, a meditative doctor who wrote much about death in the seventeenth century, when he said that 'Man is a noble animal, splendid in ashes and pompous in the grave'?

4

A Modern Search

IN THE MODERN ERA, dominated by the sciences and their practical applications in technology, some have thought that the ancient question about life after death ought not to be left to the makers of myths, to the teachers of religion, to the philosophers or to the poets. Nor should the answers be given in the form of mere beliefs. The material crying out for investigation seemed to be abundant, for 'paranormal' simply means 'beside (*para* in Greek) the normal' and, as John Schumaker pointed out in his critical study of *Wings of Illusion* (1990), 'cultural anthropologists and cross-cultural psychologists have yet to isolate a single society in which its people do not have longstanding and well-developed systems of paranormal belief'. Anecdotes galore have circulated in all the centuries and all the continents about encounters with the paranormal. But in modern times the age-old wonder has been turned into research which uses methods not completely unlike an investigation into the possibility of life on the moon or Mars. A cold, hard knife has been inserted into 'pie in the sky when you die'.

This modern concentration has been on experiences received physically, tested for their authenticity by scientific methods and if possible repeated under the controls which are standard in professionally recognized laboratories. It is thought that if human beings have 'minds' or 'spirits' which do not entirely depend on the possession of material bodies, and which are therefore capable of surviving death, it ought to be possible to prove this by experiences which are undeniably authentic encounters with reality. Such findings could be incorporated into the normal scientific world-view and it would become more easily credible that disembodied spirits could exist and could communicate with each other and with us even if 'dead'. Or so it has been hoped. And the hope remains at the end of the twentieth century. In his *Philosophy and Belief in Life after Death* (1995), R. W. K. Paterson was sympathetic with the possibility that religion may help in the search. If belief in God is presupposed, 'then the argument from divine love and mercy does strike me as providing very powerful grounds for belief in immortality, and the argument from divine justice surely provides irresistible grounds for the belief that we survive our deaths at least for some sufficient span of time'. But in his own thinking he did not make religious arguments central and it seems that part of the reason was his lack of respect for a Christianity which crudely 'envisages a Judgement, with Heaven or Hell as the destinations of different souls and a bodily resurrection'. Since the religion best known to him had provided so little credible support for the 'proposition' of immortality, he maintained that 'the probability or improbability of belief in this proposition will reflect the degree to which it is supported or undermined by the best evidence available from psychology, parapsychology, historical research, physics and perhaps other fields of empirical enquiry'.

So what have been the results of this modern search?

Emanuel Swedenborg, a Swedish scientist and engineer who died in 1772, was the most famous of the pioneers who claimed to be able to describe the conditions of the dead from direct experience. He published many accounts of visions which he said were reports of visits to another world, inhabited by the angels who taught the dead how to develop their own higher natures. People who refused to learn were sent off to hell but otherwise this world of the dead was not alarming, for here everything physical (including marriage) had an improved version which was spiritual, and in the background God presided benevolently. The dead took a kindly and active interest in the affairs of the living; for example, Swedenborg was instructed how to guide an enquirer to a hidden will which was advantageous. Some Swedenborgian churches have survived – and Swedenborg's picture of another world has also survived, at least in outline.

Around the middle of the next century, interest intensified in claims that spirits without bodies, including spirits of the dead, could communicate with the living. Spiritualism began in the excitement produced by claims that noises and disturbances caused by spirits had been experienced in the USA. Further interest was aroused by hypnotism (the creation of a trance, or state of semi-consciousness, in which buried memories and extraordinary powers of 'mind over matter' could be made public) and later by telepathy (the communication of thoughts between people who, according to natural laws, are not able to reach each other). Both these phenomena became widely accepted as real and they strengthened the belief that 'the mind' or 'the spirit' is at least in some ways and on some occasions not completely dependent on the body as (increasingly) known to modern science. Or if this belief seemed unacceptable, suggestive parallels could be drawn between the telepathic powers of humans and the body-based communications between birds, fish and animals not using language. As the decline of traditional religious beliefs in the West disturbed many, curiosity about the claims of spiritualists also became widespread. The curiosity could produce scepticism. Many 'mediums' or 'sensitives' who purported to hear and convey messages from the dead, often through raps on a table or 'spirit writing', were proved to be frauds, and questions were asked about those who were sincere: did they hypnotize themselves or others into believing that they were really in touch with the dead and did they display a surprisingly accurate knowledge about the living people around them because they had used telepathy to 'read their minds'? But the feeling was widespread that 'there may be something in it'.

Serious interest in these new developments led to the formation of the Society for Psychical Research in London in 1882. The founders included not only literary figures but also distinguished scientists and philosophers. Their initiative was copied in many other countries. (In France, for example, the most popular writer about science in the second half of the century, Camille Flammarion, was fascinated by spiritualism. So was the philosopher Henri Bergson.) The intention was to encourage investigations into 'those faculties of Man, real or supposed, which appear to be inexplicable on any generally recognized hypothesis'.

The most secure discovery was that considerable numbers of people were convinced that they had seen or felt 'apparitions' of the dead, particularly of relatives or friends who were dying or recently dead, including some who had moved many miles away or whose critical condition was for other reasons unknown to the recipients. These reports suggested something akin to an outburst of psychical energy in some of the dying, an outburst able to cross the frontiers erected by what scientists knew as natural laws. That was startling. But these reports seemed to be in a category different from the stories about ghosts which had circulated in every human society around the world. Ghost stories could be said to have begun in the imagination interpreting ordinary noises or lights, or in the desire to impress, and anyway they usually reported appearances which did not fit into people's feelings about what was 'right'. They almost always occurred by night when the reasoning powers of the living were at a low level, and in distressing circumstances such as burial grounds or places where the dead had been very unhappy. If the ghosts spoke it was almost always with complaints (about not being avenged, or not being buried properly, or not being fed after death, to give three examples) and with messages of doom and gloom. Conceivably, ghosts had somehow left behind lasting traces of their misery (before suicide, for example), but they were far less welcome than the dearly loved relatives or friends now widely believed to have made their survival, and often also their happiness, known to some of the living whom they loved. Interest in the possibility of receiving such assurance grew naturally during and after the heavy casualties in the First World War. 'We want a religion you can prove' declared Sir Arthur Conan Doyle, the creator of Sherlock Holmes and an enthusiast for investigations of the 'spirit world' much in the style used so brilliantly by that detective. A leading scientist, Sir Oliver Lodge, believed that detailed messages had come from his son Raymond, who had been killed at the Front. Many of the bereaved took a very understandable interest in this source of consolation.

But such interest declined. Clearly, some exercises of imagination by the living were involved, for often the dead 'appeared' in their normal clothes and if they 'spoke' about it described the 'other world' in terms which most people thought ludicrous or at least unconvincing. It did not seem a complete answer to say that these communications came from spirits at the elementary level of development after death, for the question could be asked why little or nothing was heard at the level of the great music, art or literature produced by humans before death. William James, a philosopher who certainly possessed what he called 'the will to believe', confessed a year before his death in 1930 that 'I am theoretically no further forward than I was at the beginning'. He was therefore 'tempted to believe that the Creator has eternally intended this part of nature to remain baffling'. Frederick Myers, an enthusiast for psychical research who coined the word 'telepathy', was believed to have sent this message from the 'other world': 'I appear to be standing behind a sheet of frosted glass which blurs sight and deadens sound, dictating feebly to a reluctant and somewhat obtuse secretary.' In Britain another discouragement was the Fraudulent Mediums Act of 1951.

So from the 1930s a keen interest was taken in the attempts by an American investigator, J. B. Rhine, and others to demonstrate 'extrasensory perception' by experiments in 'parapsychology'. Some still hoped that tests in laboratory conditions would increase confidence in the power to survive death, about which Rhine remained agnostic. The immediate purposes were, however, to examine claims about clairvoyance (the ability to perceive things beyond the range of the senses), precognition (the ability to foresee future events) and psychokinesis (the ability to alter the state of things out of reach). Typical experiments sought to prove an uncanny knowledge of, or control over, numbers, cards and dice. But again interest declined, since few members of the scientific community were willing to grant that the experiments had been conducted according to reliable standards. One reason for their reluctance was that there seemed to be too many hopes of finding evidence in favour of beliefs, instead of a completely objective investigation. Another difficulty felt was that 'positive' results did not seem to be repeatable, as they would have been after normal scientific experiments. One difficulty has been acknowledged even by those inclined to defend the reports about the 'paranormal': it is the likelihood that the involvement of a sceptic in an investigation will mean that paranormal powers cannot be exerted in the unsympathetic atmosphere. (In the USA the Committee for the Investigation of Claims of the Paranormal was ruthlessly unsympathetic from 1976.) But some wider objections have also been raised. Why are paranormal powers confined to special occasions? Why is it normally impossible to read a book without opening its covers, or to do physical work without physical effort, or to avoid disasters by accurately predicting dangers without the trouble of scientific research? And if the question about life after death is answered by a reference to 'apparitions', why do not the dead always make themselves known to those who grieve? The conclusion often drawn is that the living brain does indeed have strange powers and memories which deserve recognition and investigation, but that the matter is best left in hands of scientifically minded psychologists.

In his *Parapsychology: A Concise History* (1992) John Beloff provided a fair summary of the evidence. He was a university lecturer who, while making no claim to have had paranormal experiences himself, was 'satisfied that the basic phenomena are indeed real, not imaginary, although of course there is always room for argument as to which of the particular historical cases can be accepted at face value and which are spurious'. However, he understood why 'over the years parapsychologists have become cynical about talk of a "definitive experiment", if only because, with sufficient ingenuity, we can always think up *some* counter-explanation'. 'In the last resort,' he concluded, 'even when we can agree about the facts (which is rare enough in parascience) theoretical positions remain optional.' Just as 'normal mental activity can always be attributed to brain activity and the brain conceived as a natural computer with electrochemical neural circuits for its wiring', so telepathy can be attributed to coincidence or to shrewd observation of visible behaviour; clairvoyance and precognition to informed guesswork; and psychokinesis to mistaken observation or to fraud. Beloff sadly noted the 'virtual disappearance of strong paranormal phenomena at the present time'. He also noted the Chinese custom under Communism of classifying such phenomena as remain for investigation as 'exceptional human body function', a modest category.

For the purpose of an enquiry into the possibility of life after death, this outcome of modern psychical research seems disappointing. R. W. K. Paterson, who declared himself to be a 'diehard rationalist', has nevertheless decided that the evidence to which he appeals is sufficient to justify belief in a 'plurality of worlds, each created by small groups of interacting selves, with the possibility that an individual self may transfer from one to another according to his current state of consciousness, his character and emotional needs, and the strength of his existing and developing relationships'. But it is difficult to resist the impression that there was something personal, rather than scientific, in his defiant attitude to what he called the 'antecedent improbability' of any survival after death. Moreover, the 'other world' which he envisaged seems suspiciously like a school or university with promotion into a higher class or graduation with honours.

Interest has therefore moved on to reports of experiences more normal than those which had been investigated by psychical research. An American book of 1975 by Raymond Moody, *Life after Life*, drew world-wide attention to the frequency of experiences of 'otherworld journeys' by patients who, usually after being drugged heavily, had been pronounced clinically dead during attempts to resuscitate them in the emergency wards of hospitals (often after cardiac arrests).

Many such patients reported hearing a loud noise which might be music, seeing darkness, floating above the hospital bed, rapidly reviewing their lives with self-criticism, feeling drawn through a tunnel to a brilliant light which at first could be frightening, meeting at least one very friendly 'being of light' and being reunited with 'dead' relatives and friends, before reluctantly accepting a summons back to their bodies. On their return, patients could describe hearing the talk, and seeing the work, of the medical team during the period when they had been thought to be dead. Sometimes they could also report visiting other hospital rooms or seeing objects invisible from their beds.

Also impressive was the frequency with which many people's lives had been transformed by these experiences. People who had been competitive materialists, and often atheists, were now spiritually minded, detached from this-worldly ambitions and cares, far more tolerant, far less likely to think God hostile or dead and far less anxious about the approach of their real deaths. Here seemed to be the evidence which had been long desired, supplied without any motive for fraud and without any dubious attempt to copy tests in scientific laboratories. Paradoxically, it had come as a result of medical technology which had been suspected by some of the spiritually minded; and it had come from people who usually did not claim to be specially 'psychic'. In 1982 a Gallup poll was published which suggested that about eight million Americans had had these experiences.

Many later publications added to such reports. It was shown that these 'journeys' could be experienced by children, and also by adults who had been born blind. Nor were they made only by modern Christians who identified the 'being of light' as Jesus. Figures of Hindu gods could be seen; parallels could be drawn with *post mortem* journeys into 'the Void' reported in Buddhist texts; stories of 'otherworld journeys' by Christians in the Middle Ages or by shamans in pagan, non-modern societies were recalled; a British philosopher who remained an atheist, Sir Alfred Ayer, felt the presence of 'guardians' of space and time with the possibility that he might himself 'cure space by operating on time'. Rock-climbers who thought that they were falling to their deaths, and sailors who thought that they were drowning, have also reported a time of a strange calm while they reviewed their lives. And although most of their experiences were joyful, some resuscitated patients reported having had a fearful time, experiencing not usually the fires of traditional pictures of hell but an otherworld of condemnation, humiliation, desolation, chaos and loneliness, sometimes with acute pain. The reports which showed that different kinds of imagery were being used, and that life after death might not be entirely pleasant, seemed only to add to the authenticity of the core discovery, which was (it seemed) that death could be survived by one's spirit. As Ian Wilson put it in *Life after Death?: The Evidence* (1997), if we take these experiences seriously 'we are obliged to wander further and further into a world in which the normal bounds of what we may fondly *suppose* to be reality seem no longer to apply, and in which everything is almost literally mind-blowing'.

However, like the earlier 'findings' of psychical research, these reports can be interpreted without any conclusion that life after death is proved. It can be pointed out that most patients make no claim to have had definite experiences while believed to be dead – and that the stories of those who do make such claims may grow taller in the telling. The emphasis can be on the medical fact that these patients were, after all, not completely dead; if they heard any premature talk about their deaths during their semiconsciousness it was because the power of hearing is one of the last to go when dying. These points have often been accepted and the 'journeys' are now called 'near-death experiences' (or NDEs in the jargon of what has become a large literature), in the same category as the 'out-of-body experiences' familiar to anyone who dreams or daydreams.

The contents of these near-death dreams can be explained within the terms of medical science. Procedures during resuscitations can already be familiar to patients since they are often shown by actors in TV dramas about life in hospitals. During such crises, the brain begins to die because it is starved of oxygen: first uncontrolled hyperactivity and then 'anoxia' account for the semiconscious patient's experiences of noise and darkness. With less input reaching the brain from the senses, and with fewer inhibitions preventing the release of stored memories, what is experienced seems to be specially real although in fact it is all a dream. If the dream is pleasant, the feeling of bliss is the result of the production by a gland of adrenalin and by the brain of opiate-like chemicals known as endorphins, which are known to counteract traumatic stress in other situations; if the dream is a nightmare, that is because the pain caused by the continuing attempts at resuscitation is greater than the tranquillizing effects of the adrenalin and the endorphins. Endorphins do not usually produce hallucinations but the 'light' seen is the growing blank in the centre of the deteriorating mind's picture of reality. The 'beings' seen are memories but are entirely imaginary. The 'floating' with a bird's-eye view is an illusion, as in a dream. Or so it can be explained. What is certain is that the half-alive brain was the instrument which received every impression in these near-death experiences. They, too, might be called by the cautious Chinese 'exceptional body functions'.

It therefore appears that a belief in life after death can be strengthened by the research which has produced evidence that humans have more mental powers than they usually think – and had 'psychical research' been more seriously interested in the history of religion, this belief would have been strengthened by the demonstration that people have more spiritual powers than they usually think. The belief can also be strengthened by the many recent reports that when people are near death they can have reassuring experiences. But the decision that life after death is a real possibility must involve a belief which falls short of scientific proof because it lies outside the scope of science: it belongs not to a laboratory making experiments but to a total view of life. And so the situation remains as it did in 1553, when François Rabelais is said to have included among a number of deathbed sayings (which he may have rehearsed in advance) the famous words that he went to seek 'the great Perhaps'.

5
Traditions

IF WE ASK what has been the contribution of Christianity, we find that churches have issued 'orders' (compulsory programmes) to regulate funerals, and 'catechisms' as a basis for the instruction of their members about the meaning of death. The basic purpose has been to affirm triumph over death in words, and in actions which could have their own eloquence: from the time of the New Testament (James 5:14) the seriously sick were anointed with prayer; from a very early date the sacrament of the 'body' and 'blood' of Christ was administered to the dying as the *viaticum* for the last journey; from the fifth century sins were confessed and absolved in the final hours. While memories of persecution in the Roman Empire were still vivid, Christians wanted their dead to be buried near the tombs of the martyrs. In later ages, Christian burials were in or near churches and because burial in the consecrated churchyard, near the continuing prayers of the living, was valued so highly there was no objection to the custom of collecting bones and re-using graves. Even when the bodies have been buried or cremated at a distance, the names of the 'faithful departed' have been included in regular worship. In every period the clergy and other members of the churches have very often done all that was humanly possible to comfort the dying and the bereaved, and the funeral itself has often been remembered gratefully.

But the comfort which the churches have given to the dying and the bereaved is not the only side of the story. While humbler Christians, lay or ordained, have often been far more sensitive, the official spokesmen for the churches have often been dogmatic in ways which have come to seem, in many eyes, profoundly wrong. In their desire to persuade people not to regret leaving this world they appear to have denied what has been a basic human experience, the experience which has persuaded countless people that the world actually is a creation owing its existence to the goodness of the Creator. Despite all our complaints about the world, it seems common sense to say that it is very wonderful, very beautiful and often very good to us. And the most powerful spokesmen for the churches (who were men) do not seem to have been entirely convinced that the Creator is rightly called 'Father', for they have alleged that most of his children end up by being tortured endlessly in hell. Indeed, some have said that this was his inflexible decree about their fates even before they were born. And the teachers most honoured in the churches have seemed blind to the simplest of facts. They have denied that death follows birth as night follows day, claiming that Adam and Eve might have lived for ever had they not 'fallen'. They have claimed too that our 'souls' are little people inside our bodies – little people who at death leave the bodies behind but are later reunited with them in the 'resurrection of the flesh'. Pastoral care and official teaching have seemed to come from different churches.

First I offer a brief commentary on the 'Order for the Burial of the Dead' which provided the only fully authorized funerals in the Church of England between 1662 and 1980. A similar service was used over a long period by Anglicans outside England and, as we have noted, it was only in the nineteenth century that official provision was made for non-Anglican burials in England. I refer to this Book of Common Prayer before submitting some remarks about official Roman Catholic teaching, because as a priest in the Church of England – a happy priest – I feel an obligation to mention first criticisms frequently made of my own tradition, criticisms with which I agree. Later funeral services have been improvements, but millions have been buried or have mourned to the sound of these words, and this Prayer Book has had a huge influence on reactions to what it called 'the daily spectacle of our mortality'.

The service included no Eucharist in which Christians could be reminded that Jesus himself died. This omission was in deliberate contrast with the custom of medieval Catholicism, which was to hold one Requiem Mass before the funeral and three in the month after it, with an *obit* as a Mass in commemoration each year while wanted. From the ninth century, the Church had operated an ordered series of actions and words which had been as near as humankind has ever got to the taming of death. But that whole great system of consolation and hope had been hastily buried by the Protestant Reformers as soon as they had obtained the power to order what words and actions were to be used in the public life of the Church. Strong reasons were given for this drastic change. There was a theological protest against doctrines and prayers which seemed to claim that the Church had the right and the ability to control what happened to people after their deaths, but at least as influential was the protest against the practical effects of a system which had been for the benefit of the clergy who had operated it: priests received fees for Masses, many of them (the 'chantry priests') lived solely or mainly on endowments for the perpetual offering of Masses, and above all the clergy had the prestige of the ability to handle the keys to heaven or hell, resulting in many solid privileges on earth. For some, the Protestant Reformation was a revolt in the name of God the one Judge; for others, it was a revolt by some of the laity. But one result was to deprive most of the laity of the traditional forms of consolation when death had struck.

The Prayer Book service included no acknowledgement of the grief of the mourners with a prayer that they might be comforted; instead they were told 'not to be sorry'. It did not arrange for any informal words to be spoken in an attempt to relate the death to the personality of the deceased or to the feelings of those gathered in remembrance. It quoted from the Book of Job 'the Lord gave and the Lord hath taken away', apparently denying that any death could be accidental or against the will of God, but it did not do what probably many of the mourners wanted it to do, for it did not repeat from the service for the 'Visitation of the Sick' words which might have been thought appropriate at the burial. These were simple words of trust in God's mercy: 'We humbly commend the soul of this thy servant . . . into thy hands, as into the hands of a faithful Creator and most merciful Saviour.' To commend the sick to God was still correct but to commend the dead was now said to be contrary to Holy Scripture. In a diplomatic compromise, the funeral service authorized for Lutherans in Sweden in 1525 prayed 'if this our departed brother be in such a condition that our prayers can avail for his soul'. But in England the Book of Common Prayer was less merciful to the mourners because its compilers were so determined to get rid of what they regarded as abuses in the medieval system.

Probably the main impact of the service was to present an austere, even gloomy view of human life and of its Creator, in striking contrast with the early Christian emphasis on triumph and joy. A tone which would have been in place when rebuking the flippant was used when dealing with mourners. Words were taken from the Scriptures and other traditional sources:

> Verily every man living is altogether vanity. For man walketh in a vain shadow, and disquieteth himself in vain . . . Take thy plague away from me: I am even consumed by means of thy heavy hand . . . Though men be strong that they come to fourscore years: yet is their strength then but labour and sorrow, so soon passeth it away, and we are gone . . . Man that is born of a woman hath but a short time to live and is full of misery. He cometh up and is cut down, like a flower; he fleeth as it were a shadow, and never continueth in one stay. In the midst of life we are in death: of whom may we seek for succour but of thee, O Lord, who for our sins art justly displeased?

Human flesh was called a 'burden' and 'vile' and 'hearty thanks' were offered that it had pleased God to 'deliver' the dead 'from the miseries of this sinful world'.

Such hope as was offered by this funeral was for church members in good standing. The service was not to be used for 'any that die unbaptized, or excommunicated, or have laid violent hands on themselves'. It was therefore not a means of consoling the parents of an infant who had died before baptism was possible, nor was any alternative provided, and the belief was common that such infants could never be admitted to heaven. Similarly, Christians who had been excommunicated (perhaps for a failure to pay 'tithes', a tenth of their crops, to the clergy) were excluded, as of course were all 'Jews, Turks, heretics and infidels' (in the words of the prayer appointed for use on Good Friday). All suicides were also excluded, whatever might have been their mental state.

The hope held out to those whose bodies were buried with the words 'earth to earth, ashes to ashes, dust to dust' was that after a 'rest' in 'sleep', or in 'joy and felicity', they would be resurrected. The Book of Job (19:26, 27) was quoted in a translation which made that tormented man declare: 'I know that my Redeemer liveth, and that he shall stand at the latter day upon the earth. And although after my skin worms destroy this body, yet in my flesh shall I see God.' Until 1662, in 1549 and later editions, an older translation had been used: 'I shall rise out of the earth in the last day, and shall be covered again with my own skin, and shall see God in my flesh: yea, and I myself shall behold him, and not with other, but with these same eyes.' But as was noted in (for example) the Oxford Study Edition of the New English Bible (1976), 'these verses have been so poorly preserved that it is impossible to discern their exact meaning'. All that is clear is that 'Job expresses his certainty that somehow and somewhere he will be shown to have been innocent'.

Many passages in the Book of Job do not expect this vindication to come after death. On the contrary, death is a further disaster for

> If I look to the grave as my house,
> if I spread my couch in darkness,
> if I call the pit my father
> or if I call the worm my mother or sister,
> where is my hope? (17:13–15)

> As clouds break up and disperse,
> so the man who goes down to the grave never returns,
> he never goes home again
> and his place will know him no more. (7:9–10)

When Job receives some sort of an answer to his protests at the end of the book, it is through a vision of the wonders of the natural world, and an epilogue which seems to have been added later is a happy inventory of his recovered wealth. There is no talk about the vision of God in eternity, for Job's vindication must be in 'his place', on earth, before death. Thus the hope offered by the Book of Job is the opposite of the hope offered by the Prayer Book, for it seems that what Job was said to hope for was not resurrection after death but a recovery of health, not because he will be forgiven but because he has always been innocent.

This funeral was constructed around the 'sure and certain hope' that a good and faithful Christian's body would become like Christ's glorious body 'at the general Resurrection in the last day'. In the Articles of Religion which set out some of the doctrines of the Church of England, Christ's body was said to be 'with flesh, bones and all things pertaining to the perfection of Man's nature'. When Christ rose from death he 'took again his body . . . wherewith he ascended into Heaven, and there sitteth'. But church members would have to be firmly orthodox if they were to be given this resurrection. The 'Creed of St Athanasius' (in fact a document from the turn of the fourth and fifth centuries which summarized the teaching of St Augustine) was ordered to be used at Christmas and Easter and on a dozen other great days in the Church's year. It predicted that anyone disagreeing with its definition of the Catholic Faith would without doubt 'perish everlastingly', joining all 'they that have done evil' in 'everlasting fire'.

In this funeral a prayer begged the Father: 'suffer [allow] us not, at our last hour, for any pains of death to fall from thee'. This prayer might be interpreted as a petition to be spared 'pains of death' so intense that a lifetime of faith in God was replaced by agony, despair and disbelief, ignoring the continuing presence and activity of God. But it could easily be understood as saying that if there was misbehaviour on the deathbed, God would allow the culprit to 'fall' outside his love. When so understood, this prayer might seem to suggest that the Father was indignant to hear the cry of the dying Jesus, 'My God, my God, why have you forsaken me?' (the only cry from the cross reported in the gospels of Mark and Matthew), but evidently it was thought possible that the Father might not forgive the wrong sort of reaction when near death, for he seemed to be a Father who found forgiveness hard. As the Articles of Religion taught, Christ 'truly suffered, was crucified, dead and buried' (indeed, 'went down into Hell') because that was needed 'to reconcile his Father to us' – not in order to reconcile us to the Father, which was the biblical teaching.

Even a strict orthodoxy untainted by any misbehaviour when dying would not be enough for the salvation of a Christian whose name was not among those 'predestined' or 'elected' to enter heaven. The idea that God predetermines or knows what has not yet occurred convinced many Christians in the past but has almost always come to seem nonsensical, for the simple reason that the future is not there to be known. Many things in Nature are unpredictable, from the behaviour of elementary particles upwards – and so are many things in life. To the believer, it now almost always seems clear that the creation of a world full of freedom and novelty has pleased the Creator. But this Prayer Book service asked God 'shortly to accomplish the number of thine elect' so that the history which was the preparation of the non-elect for hell could be concluded. The Articles of Religion explained that:

> Predestination to Life is the everlasting purpose of God, whereby (before the foundations of the world were laid) he hath constantly decreed by his own counsel secret to us, to deliver from curse and damnation those whom he hath chosen in Christ out of mankind, and to bring them by Christ to everlasting salvation, as vessels made to honour.

The Articles warned 'curious and carnal persons' not to be sure that God had predestined them to hell for that might 'thrust them either into desperation, or into wretchedness of most unclean living', but even this form of predestination, to everlasting fire, was not called an impossibility.

The Articles were clearer in teaching that although 'good works which are the fruits of faith . . . are pleasing and acceptable to God in Christ', 'works done before the grace of Christ, and the inspiration of his Spirit, are not pleasant to God'. Thus 'they also are to be held accursed that presume to say, That every man shall be saved by the Law or Sect which he professeth, so that he be diligent to frame his life according to that Law and the light of Nature'. To sum up: heaven was reserved for predestined Christians.

Before condemning these beliefs, we should note that in the seventeenth century the authorities in the Church of England were under pressure from the Puritans (extreme Protestants) to abandon any prayer voicing hope for the particular person whose body was being buried, since the soul of this person might already have been condemned by God to the everlasting pains of hell. Indeed, all prayers for the dead were thought to be either offensive to the Judge who had made this decision, or else superfluous since the dead were already in heaven or hell; therefore it would be best not to have any words at all at the burial. When the Church of England had been temporarily overthrown in the 1640s, the victorious Puritans issued a *Directory for the Public Worship of God* which ordered that the dead body should be 'decently attended to the place appointed for public burial, and there immediately interred, without any ceremony'. There might be sermons in church after funerals, but even these were prohibited by the General Assembly of the Church of Scotland in 1638. The Puritans who emigrated to New England, although they allowed sermons after a burial, were very slow to allow any words to be spoken during it. The Puritan character had great moral strengths: the vision of God as majestic and holy, the acknowledgement of evil in humanity, the conviction that life is a serious affair with a momentous outcome, the insistence that in religion a genuine faith must be a personal decision, and energy. But it is significant that not even in New England, which was purer than Old England, could funerals be forgotten. The emotion was too firmly rooted in human nature: people wished to express in spoken words the hope that the great God would share the love of mourners for their fellow humans, sinful as they must be and mysterious as must be their destiny.

Some or many of the ideas clothed in powerful words by the Book of Common Prayer will seem strange, even offensive, to almost all Anglicans in the twenty-first century, for a more cheerful view has been taken of life before death and of life after it, because the emphasis has been on the goodness of the Creator who gives life and sustains it. It has become customary for Anglican theologians to explain the belief in the 'resurrection of the body' required by the Apostles' Creed as referring not to our present flesh but to what will be needed, in a way as yet unknown, for a person's 'expression and activity'. This has been taught in reports from the Doctrine Commission of the Church of England.

But thinking of heaven in more spiritual terms has not meant making it less heavenly: it has been seen as union with the glory of God. And because the most glorious thing about God has been seen to be his love, it has been believed that there is a wideness in his mercy. In practice, Anglican clergy in England have thought it right to conduct very many funerals of people who, if baptized, have not shown much awareness of the obligations of the baptized: they, too, have been entrusted 'to the mercy of God our Maker and Redeemer'. There have still been hesitations or objections about the expression of hopes for non-Christians or prayers for the Christian dead. In the Alternative Service Book of the Church of England (1980), prayer was offered at the funeral only for 'the whole Church, living and departed in the Lord Jesus', and at Holy Communion the prayer was only that God would 'grant us with them' ('those who have died in the faith of Christ') 'a share in your eternal Kingdom'. But many funerals have not been confined to the officially authorized words and many prayers have voiced the simple hope that all the dead may rest in peace. And, as one of the alternatives allowed within this Alternative Service Book of 1980, it was permitted to pray for 'those whose faith is known to you alone' yet who have 'died in the peace of Christ'. It was also permitted to 'commend all who have died to your unfailing love, that in them your will may be fulfilled'. Thus there has been change from the atmosphere in the Book of Common Prayer.

The same emphasis on the love of God, and therefore on hope, is very clear in the wording of funerals authorized in the Roman Catholic Church since the Second Vatican Council in the 1960s. The *Order of Christian Funerals*, issued with authority in 1990, is full of pastoral sensitivity as it offers a wide variety of services to be held in the home, in the church or in the crematorium, and provision is made for choice in the selection of prayers from a collection which takes account of many possible emotions and needs. In a recent collection of essays – *Interpreting Death* edited by Peter Jupp and Tony Rogers (1997) – the presentation of this *Order* was made by a parish priest who is also an expert of liturgy, and was entitled 'Celebrating our journey into Christ'. But recent authoritative teaching can be heard, at least by suspicious critics, as having a different tone. It is harder to expect the teaching in the *Catechism of the Catholic Church* (1992) to be altered by the Roman Catholic authorities. But the early responses to this official publication showed that not all members or theologians of that Church shared the stern certainties of the catechism and it seems likely that pressure for its revision will grow.

Some clarifications or developments of doctrine in this catechism have already been widely praised. For example, there has been a welcome for the firm teaching that all may pray 'count us among those you have chosen' since 'God predestines no one to go to hell' (1037). But some of the catechism has seemed more questionable.

As in much past teaching in almost all the Christian traditions, the starting point is the hope of resurrection of a small minority of humankind, communicant members of the Church. 'It is Jesus himself who will raise up those who have believed in him, who have eaten his body and drunk his blood' (994). 'Believing in Jesus Christ and the One who sent him for our salvation is necessary for obtaining that salvation' (161). And again the resurrection expected is physical. Death is the 'separation of the soul from the body', and 'the Church teaches that every spiritual soul is created immediately by God – it is not "produced" by parents – and also that it is immortal: it does not perish when it separates from the body at death, and it will be reunited with the body at the final Resurrection' (336). In death 'the human body decays and the soul goes to meet God, while awaiting its reunion with its glorified body' (997). The end will be 'the true resurrection of this flesh which we now possess' (1017). It will include 'all the dead' and will occur in connection with the Last Judgement but this great assize at the end of history will only confirm what has already been decided about each person 'at the very moment of each person's death'. Now 'death puts an end to human life as the time open to either accepting or rejecting the divine grace manifested in Christ' (1021–2), yet death could have been avoided. 'The Church's *Magisterium*, as the authentic interpreter of the affirmations of Scripture and Tradition, teaches that death entered the world on account of man's sin' and that 'man would have been immune from bodily death had he not sinned' (1008).

In all these teachings the catechism echoes what has been taught very widely in the history of Christianity. But some passages repeat doctrines which are more specifically Roman Catholic definitions.

The condition to which 'the Church gives the name Purgatory' is explained: 'All who die in God's grace and friendship, but still imperfectly purified, are indeed assured of their eternal salvation, but after death they undergo purification, so as to achieve the holiness necessary to enter heaven' (1030). 'The tradition of the Church, by reference to certain texts of Scripture, speaks of a cleansing fire' even for those souls being prepared for heaven, and the catechism warns that people guilty of mortal or deadly sin, defined as 'a wilful turning away from God' with 'persistence in it until the end' (1037), will suffer 'immediate and everlasting damnation'. The warning is very clear and very solemn: 'To die in mortal sin without repenting and accepting God's merciful love means remaining separated from him for ever by our own free choice', so that 'immediately after death the souls of those who die in a state of mortal sin descend into hell, where they suffer the punishments of hell, "eternal fire"' (1033–5).

Later in this catechism it is explained that 'for a sin to be mortal, three conditions must together be met: 'Mortal sin is sin whose object is a grave matter and which is also committed with full knowledge and deliberate consent' (1857). 'Grave matter' includes blasphemy, the prohibition of which 'extends to language against Christ's Church, the saints and sacred things' (2148). 'The faithful are obliged to participate in the Eucharist on days of obligation, unless excused for a serious reason' and 'those who deliberately fail in this obligation commit a grave sin' (2181). 'Days of obligation' include all Sundays and 'feast' days (1389). Since 'grave matter is specified by the Ten Commandments' (1858) and 'voluntary doubt about the faith' is condemned in the exposition of the first Commandment, it seems possible that an example of sin which deserves hell is 'the doubt which disregards or refuses to hold as true what God has revealed and the Church proposes for belief' (2088). It is stressed that 'Jesus often speaks of "Gehenna", of the "unquenchable fire" reserved for those who to the end of their lives refuse to believe and to be converted, where both body and soul can be lost' (1035). However, the catechism adds that although 'we can judge that an act is in itself a grave offence, we must entrust the judgement of persons to the justice and mercy of God' (1861).

Probably many reactions to what is taught in this *Catechism of the Catholic Church* would depend on what weight is given to some passages which convey a gentler impression.

In 1979 the Sacred Congregation for the Doctrine of Faith issued a warning from the Vatican: 'neither the Bible nor the theologians give us sufficient light to enable us to give a proper description of the life which is to come after death', so that we must await the 'dispensation of full light'. Some passages in the catechism seem to be fully in keeping with the humble spirit which the Sacred Congregation then recommended. For example, while it is inevitable and proper that Christians should see Christ the Saviour at the centre of their hopes about life after death, it is taught that the possibility of salvation of non-Christians need not be denied. Quoting the Second Vatican Council (although in small print) the catechism says that 'those who through no fault of their own, do not know the Gospel of Christ or his Church, but who nevertheless seek God with a sincere heart, and, moved by his grace, try in their actions to do his will as they know it through the dictates of their conscience – these too may achieve eternal salvation' (847).

The very close relationship, even the unity, of the soul with the body need not be denied. Indeed, the catechism itself makes this point, reminding us that 'in Sacred Scripture the word "soul" often refers to the innermost aspect of man, that which is of the greatest value to him, that by which he is most especially in God's image; "soul" signifies the spiritual principle in man' (363). And this understanding of 'soul' is reflected in the teaching that 'the unity of body and soul is so profound that one has to consider the soul to be the form of the body: i.e., it is because of its spiritual soul that the body becomes a living, human body; spirit and matter, in man, are not two natures united but rather their union forms a single nature' (365).

More strangely, the emphasis on the unity of body and soul inspires the doctrine of the resurrection of 'this flesh which we now possess'. But it is also said that our resurrected bodies will need to be 'changed' and 'glorified' by being made 'spiritual'. Moreover, 'the "how" of this change exceeds our imagination and understanding; it is accessible only to faith' (1000). And although the teaching about the connection between death and human sin is based on the story about Adam and Eve as used by St Paul, and it is said that the story 'affirms a primeval event', it is also taught that the story 'uses figurative language' (390).

The teaching about specified 'grave' sins which, unless repented before death, result in condemnation to hell is indeed stern, but it contrasts favourably with the harsher doctrine of John Calvin that 'all sin is mortal' – a doctrine which supports the strict Calvinist's belief that God is being just when he predestines almost the whole of humanity to hell, since everyone not only inherits Adam's 'original' sin but also has committed at least one sin personally, thus deserving eternal death and fire. Like other Protestants, Calvin rejected any idea about 'purgatory': to him there was the one alternative, heaven or hell.

It may, however, be questioned whether this catechism does justice to the utter solemnity of the traditional picture of the Last Judgement, since now the so-called 'judgement' seems to have become no more than the confirmation and wider publication of what has already been decided and made known to each person 'at the very moment of each person's death'. The saints – who have not needed purification, or who have 'achieved' it – 'take up their bodies again' but since they have already been living 'in the celestial paradise with Christ, joined to the company of the holy angels' (1023), it is not easy to see what they gain by becoming once more physical. If those who are 'condemned' receive back their bodies only in order that the pain of punishments in hell may be increased, this belief seems to encourage not trust in his justice and mercy but questioning about the moral character, or sanity, of the Judge.

In an age when most people are fully aware that devout Christians have been, and remain, only a small minority in humankind as a whole, the catechism's agnosticism about the prospects in eternity of the great majority scarcely seems good news to be proclaimed to the world in the hope that it will be believed. And in an age when most people are aware of the physical basis of personality, the catechism's teaching that a person's soul is 'not produced by the parents' and 'separates from the body at death' is hard to reconcile with what is known about the formation of the human personality with its physical basis originating in the parents' intercourse. If a soul is immediately added to the sex – an idea which could be treated with levity – we may ask about the divine purpose in permitting the natural termination of a large proportion of pregnancies through miscarriages. Without life after birth, can they have life after death? If the soul is something which is detached from the body at death, we may ask what happens to the elements in the personality which did result from what the parents provided.

Further, it is incompatible with scientific biology to teach that 'death entered the world' through human sin. Complex forms of life have always died, and before they died have always depended on killing and eating other living creatures, unless they were vegetarians. And to teach that 'our present flesh' will be resurrected after death is to say something which most modern people will not reckon to be a real possibility. Each human body is indeed a *miraculum* in the original meaning of that word: it is a wonder. Its development on this planet needed 4,000 million years of evolving life. Each human body contains 100 million living cells. The chief marvels are the genes (perhaps 100,000 of them) which make the body by making proteins, and the brain with its thousands of millions of neurons. To ask for this *miraculum* to be repeated and surpassed by a 'resurrection of the flesh' when our time and space are no more seems to be asking for a marvel beyond the bounds of what is believable.

The catechism's teaching about 'grave' or 'mortal' sin stresses that such a sin has to be 'turning away from God' (nothing less) by an act of the will (not by an unavoidable response to circumstances). It has to be committed with full knowledge (of its nature and consequences) and persisted in until death (not the result of a temptation which seems overwhelming at the time). But it may be questioned why the catechism mentions in this connection sins which seem to be at a different level of gravity. Such sins include criticizing the Church, missing Mass on a Sunday without a good excuse, and the inability to believe one of the Church's teachings.

We shall return to some of these questions, but the conclusion to be drawn from a study of documents such as the old Anglican funeral service or the new *Catechism of the Catholic Church* appears to be that much (not everything) in traditional teaching needs to be revised. That seems to be the essential first step before there can be a convincing restatement of the unchanging Christian belief that the most important meaning of death for humans is that a share in the eternal life of God can lie beyond the inescapable process of dying. I am therefore one of those who are persuaded that the real situation was well described by John Macquarrie in his book on 'eschatology' (thought about the last things), *Christian Hope* (1978):

> Attempts by theologians even down to modern times to sort out all the elements in the conventional understanding of the Christian hope remind one of the endless modifications and refinements that were made in the Ptolemaic system of astronomy until finally it was abandoned for the vastly simpler Copernican scheme. Something like a Copernican revolution seems to be demanded in Christian eschatology.

6

Real Possibilities

WHAT OUGHT TO BE the thrust of such a revolution? Professor Macquarrie outlined what seems to be the right answer by asking another question: 'Could we suppose that our destiny as individuals is not to live on as immortal souls or to be provided with new bodies, but to be summed up or gathered up in the experience of God as the people we are or have been in our several segments of time and in our bodies?'

As Macquarrie is well aware, the belief that there is a real possibility of any future for people when their bodies have died needs to be related to what we now know about our dependence on our bodies.

What has been demonstrated is, it seems, that while we are alive in our bodies all our perceptions, thoughts and desires involve electrochemical movements in the brain. As William James put it, they do not come from 'a soul which is nowhere'. As Gilbert Ryle argued in his vastly influential *The Concept of Mind* (1949), there is 'no ghost in the machine'. What Thomas Hobbes wrote in *Leviathan* (1651) has been vindicated by what we now know: 'There is no conception in a man's mind which hath not at first been begotten upon the organs of the sense.'

Richard Swinburne therefore appears to be mistaken when he argues in *The Evolution of the Soul* (1986) that our mental life is 'quite different' from the physical events in our brains, so that 'there are two parts to man (and to many other animals) – a body and a soul or mind'. He grants that 'under normal mundane conditions the functioning of the soul requires the functioning of the body' but he insists that 'a man consists of his soul together with whatever, if any, body is connected with it'. He seems to be in error because while it is obviously true that our mental life ('mind') influences our physical condition and behaviour ('matter'), it is also indisputable that if we are to behave in any manner, signals from the brain must first convey instructions to the body, often releasing chemicals which change our moods. While it is also obviously true that we form thoughts and wishes in our mental life which are not exclusively determined by events in our bodies, it is also indisputable that we need bodies if we are to communicate these thoughts or carry out these wishes. Even telepathy cannot escape being physical, since it is brain-to-brain contact.

But to accept such truths in the theory of 'physicalism' does not mean that we are forced to agree with the crude version of that theory expounded by a distinguished scientist, Francis Crick, in *The Astonishing Hypothesis: The Scientific Search for the Soul* (1994). 'You, your joys and your sorrows, your memories and your ambitions, your sense of personal identity and free will, are in fact', he tells us, 'no more than the behaviour of a vast assembly of nerve cells and their associated molecules.' It is indeed astonishing that a scientist whose mental life has been so brilliant that (with James Watson) he explained the structure of the biological basis of life, DNA, in 1952 should now attempt to contradict the common sense of humanity. Almost all of us are fully aware that our joys, sorrows, memories, ambitions, personal identity and free will – and such science as we are capable of – are different from physical events, although not so different as Swinburne maintains. Crick's one-eyed view of life which reduces the mental to the physical is contrary to human experience.

Mental events are physical brainwaves but are also something more – the something which we indicate when we call a clever person 'brainy'. For the past 45,000 years or so, *Homo sapiens* has been able to sharpen and develop the rudimentary mental events which seem to occur in many other species by the acquisition of the power of language using words, for accurate thinking is silent speech. We know that we think in words, and we know what we think, because we know ourselves; and from the behaviour of others we deduce that they do much the same thing. Later we acquire other languages: we use numbers, we combine musical notes, we create symbols. Of course we seldom ignore our bodies, but almost all adults reckon that our mental, emotional and spiritual life is the most important thing about us. That is why in the past very clever thinkers were able to speak in a way which has been ridiculed as talk about a 'ghost in the machine', for they knew that introspection does appear to introduce us to a person who is in control of the body, rather as nowadays a driver is in control of a car. There is no such detachable person in reality but the long history of the theory of dualism arises from the fact that in everyday experience it often feels as if there is. Moreover, we can think about things which go beyond the control of the body, as if we could jump out of the car: we can think about the past and the future which do not now exist, in the present we imagine alternatives to what does exist, and we can ascend high into the worlds of music and art, mathematics, advanced physics, ethics and religion. And some of us are so clever that we can make computers do much of the work of our brains.

Many mental events are non-spatial in the sense that time is non-spatial although it is 'told' from the position of hands on a clock, or in the sense that music is, although it is made by solid instruments including throats. Time and the clock, music and the orchestra, have different functions although they both depend on a physical basis, much as artificial intelligence depends on a computer which needs to be assembled as something physical and which can be destroyed. Mental and physical events are, it seems, best understood as two levels of existence, being somewhat different although never detached before death. The brain is a physical structure and the mind is the process which the brain makes possible.

The marvel is what the brain of *Homo sapiens* can do. It originates when an egg with a diameter of 0.005 inches is fertilized by just one in a tumultuous onrush of sperms; it is only 2.5 per cent of the body's weight; it is not thought beautiful to look at although it enables us to see beauty; it was thrown away by the Egyptians when (around 1500 BC) they thought that they were improving their methods of embalming distinguished persons' corpses with a view to immortality; it was dismissed in favour of the heart or the lungs when the Ancient Greeks guessed where *psyche* had its centre; boxers damage it as a sport; yet without it the development of this little thing *Homo sapiens* would still be *Homo erectus*, able to work, to kill, to eat and to copulate, but not to do a great deal else. With it, *Homo sapiens* has become king of this planet, spreading out (it seems, from Africa) with an astounding speed and extent of success. On the brain depend the power and the glory of our mental events – and of the emotional and spiritual realities to which the word 'soul' refers in common speech, as when we enjoy 'soul music' or complain that someone 'has no soul'.

But is it really possible for another marvel to be this human animal's survival of death? Can our souls be saved? Or did David Hume write true words in the eighteenth century? 'The weakness of the body and that of the mind in infancy', he wrote, 'are exactly proportional; their vigour in manhood, their sympathetic disorder in sickness, their common gradual decay in old age. The step further seems unavoidable: their common dissolution in death.'

It is widely agreed we should not look to brain science for an answer although we can hope that great progress will be made in discovering how physical and mental events are related in the body before death. Francis Crick observes that at present 'consciousness is a subject about which there is little consensus, even as to what the problem is'. He will surely be given general applause when he says that 'what I want to know is what is going on in my brain when I see something' and the applause would continue if he investigated the process of thinking. 'To understand ourselves', he writes, 'we must understand how nerve cells behave and how they interact', also 'the atoms, ions and molecules that make them up and influence them.' Because such scientific investigations could yield precise results verifiable by further experiments, it is understandable why he is scornful of religion: 'if revealed religions have revealed anything, it is that they are usually wrong'. 'If the members of a church really believe in life after death', he asks, 'why do they not conduct sound experiments to establish it?'

No doubt Crick, being highly intelligent, knows when he is being serious that it is not the function of religion to conduct its own scientific investigations and experiments: its aim over many centuries has been to help us to 'understand ourselves' by other methods, including the investigation of claims that there can be contact with the divine. Almost everyone accepts this, whether or not the teachings of a particular religion are accepted. But religion is a human activity (it resembles science in this) and one of its tragedies has been that (unlike good science) it has often claimed an authority which goes beyond experience. It has been right to use myths in order to indicate experience and reflection, but religion has taken myths literally; it has been right to use symbols, but it has treated them as ultimate realities; it has been right to use speculations in order to explore the logical consequences of what it has found, but it has pretended that these are statements of facts which are known. All religion depends on beliefs which cannot be proved to be true but which are thought to be real possibilities, not contrary to what is known. Beliefs can be of supreme importance to genuine believers: to them, a belief is an idea in the light of which one is prepared to live and die without being certain.

Under such challenges, what have Christians to say?

It has become clear to many that Christianity, a tradition which has developed many beliefs which have become incredible, now needs to provide for all who look to it an interpretation of death which is in closer contact with reality. That is not impossible, for such a renewal of the tradition would have at its centre the story of Jesus, who was anxious about death and who died. 'I have a baptism to undergo, and what stress I am under, until the ordeal is over!' (Luke 12:50). He did not expect his followers to welcome death. 'Can you drink the cup that I am to drink?' (Matthew 20:22). When he saw that he must drink and die, 'horror and dismay came over him and he said to them, "My heart is ready to break with grief"' (Mark 14:33, 34). Then 'his sweat was like clots of blood falling to the ground' (Luke 22:44). It is rightly said that the unique intensity of the conviction of Jesus that God was his Father and the Father of all meant a unique intensity of suffering when dying in agony at the hands of his fellow men brought the feeling that God had forsaken him. The story of Jesus includes the terrible reality of death and so the central symbol of Christianity is the instrument of torture on which Jesus died.

This story is best recalled in the way he commanded, namely in the Eucharist (the Liturgy, the Mass, the Lord's Supper, Holy Communion), an act of remembrance of that death (and much more) which is specially significant when someone else's death is a piercing fact. However, not every dying person or every bereaved family wishes for a funeral in that form, which even deeply convinced Christians are likely to find alien if they have expressed their faith through a Protestant tradition. There are special difficulties when the funeral takes place in a crematorium within a strictly limited time. So a service which is not the Eucharist will often have to be the occasion when it has to be said by words and actions that a Christian is being taken by death into a closer identification with Christ in his death and in his eternal life. Such a funeral completes the Christian life 'on earth' which the other great sacrament, baptism, began. St Paul reminded the Christians in Rome that 'when we were baptized into union with Christ we were baptized into his death': they 'lay dead' (for a few moments, as if drowned in cold water) 'in order that, as Christ was raised from the dead in the splendour of the Father, we might begin to walk upon the new way of life' (6:3, 4). And in some situations which would have surprised St Paul – in Britain at the end of the twentieth Christian century, for example – the clergy may well feel it right to respond to a request to 'take' the funeral of someone who was never baptized. Then it may also seem right to use words other than those authorized for use after the deaths of the baptized. But in that case, too, those who mourn have a right to be reminded of the Christ who, in order to communicate the mercy of God, was not exclusive in the company he kept while he lived or when he died.

The relevance of Christ to the dead person and to the mourners needs to be explored in a way which is fresh on every occasion, but the central theme will be an explanation of why the child of God who is dead can now be entrusted to 'a faithful Creator and most merciful Saviour' because the mystery of death is now not totally mysterious. As a life on earth ends, it is surely right to give thanks for the creation of the earth and for all the goodness of the life made possible on this planet with energy pouring from the sun. If this particular life has on the whole not been happy enough to suggest that it was a gift from a good Creator, or if the extent of God's love has not been made known because the local religion does not teach it, surely that is not the end of the story. God's saving love will be made known to each one of his children at the moment of death which is the moment of entry into eternity, the Easter offered to every human life. Absolutely no one will be denied that opportunity to know this love as the ultimate reality, beyond all tragedy and above all ignorance. That is one great reason why the Christian message is 'good news' which deserves to be shared. But it is also good news for those of us whose lives, and whose access to religion, have been happier because more privileged. In those favourable situations we can still make a mess of our lives by God's standards, so that we too need the promise of transformation, the promise that 'when he is revealed we shall be like him, for we shall see him as he is' (1 John 3:2).

What then is 'faith'? Paul was surely right to remind the Christians in Rome that it is part of the essential message of Christianity to say that every individual who comes into a life-giving relationship with the true God must be 'justified by faith'. The trouble is that the words 'justified' and 'faith', although they have been the subjects of much learned or abusive discussion in the history of

Christian theology, do not now convey to most people the meaning which they had for Paul. But it seems possible, and loyal to Paul, to say very simply that 'justification' is God's action by which he first treats the sinner as not a sinner and then makes the sinner less of a sinner. And 'faith' is equally necessary if the sinner is to be transformed, for it is the response by trust in God's reality and goodness. What has been 'disclosed' is, as Paul told the Romans (3:22), 'the righteousness of God' (his unexpected form of righteousness, which is merciful). To accept that this has been disclosed requires faith in Jesus Christ, 'through whom we have been admitted to the sphere of God's grace in which we stand' (5:2). But to trust that Christ is the focus of God's self-disclosure involves more than saying to him 'Lord, Lord' (Matthew 7:21). It means our agreement to be 'changed', a key word for Paul. If this simple understanding is correct, it seems clear that both the justification and the faith have to continue and develop after death. The deathbed must be the turning point in the human response, but if it ends all possibility of change, no human being has any hope of standing in eternity.

And what is 'eternity'? The word has been given many different meanings but it has frequently been said that it is either 'timeless' or 'everlasting' and after the long history of the discussion it seems that neither of these meanings is the best.

Eternity is clearly different from the space and time which we know, so that it was nonsense to draw maps of it or to date it by years and days. That may seem a point so obvious that it does not need to be stated, yet religion has contradicted it by growing a jungle of mythology, as philosophy has done by building the castles in the air resting on cloudy intellectual systems called metaphysics ('after physics'). And many attempts have been made to employ physics in the service of mythology or metaphysics. The physics of Aristotle was used by medieval theologians, and the physics of Newton by himself as a theologian. With the concept of 'space-time' Einstein taught the twentieth century that there is no such thing as universal time, for every object is fundamentally energy and has its own time as it moves through space. He was also a pioneer in the exploration of the quantum world, where solid space is dissolved into sub-atomic particles whose movements can be measured only by statistics suggesting probability (although he himself disliked the interpretation that 'God plays dice'). But this universe where everything is moving in relation to everything else is our old universe seen at a new depth: it is not what we try to think about if we try to speak about life after death, as this is glimpsed from our inescapable standpoint of life before death. Life after death must be life in eternity, and in eternity there can be no time (or times) when events happen in a way familiar to us, as there can be no space where objects large or small move, for eternity cannot be our time continued or our space expanded. That simple truth uproots many jungles of mythology and demolishes many castles sustained by metaphysics.

Yet if we have reasons to believe that eternity is more than one of our false ideas, we have to try to think and speak about it in terms of the time and space which we know. It therefore seems to be better represented not by a total blank (suggesting that it is completely timeless) nor by a continuous straight line (suggesting that it is everlasting) but by the art of the ancient Celts (and of other peoples). They carved or painted endlessly intertwining lines or put innumerable dots on a page. Such art may help us to remember the moments in our lives when it has seemed that 'time stands still', that time has had an intensity and a significance far greater than anything which can be coldly recorded on modern watches and clocks. To be frank, these are moments of ecstatic joy which include sexual orgasm, appropriately since that can be the beginning of the wonder of a new human life. But they also include the most sublime experiences of 'the eternal now' reported by the great mystics. Much evidence suggests that many – it may be, almost all – people have had some such experiences. They can be triggered by a wide variety of occasions including overwhelming joy when beholding natural beauty or when a child is born. They are moments which are 'sacred' in the sense of being mysterious gifts and revelations to us, the most meaningful minutes or seconds in our existence, hinting (or teaching) that our lives are, after all, not pointless. Insofar as these moments can be put into words, we may use those of the Christian philosopher Boethius: 'the complete and perfect possession of unlimited life all at once'. Or we may find more meaning in the famous images of a Christian poet, William Blake:

> To see a World in a Grain of Sand,
> And a Heaven in a Wild Flower,
> Hold Infinity in the palm of your hand,
> And Eternity in an hour.

However, perhaps the greatest music says it best and the greatest art conveys more about the intensity of this beauty than words can.

But we have not finished our questioning, for these glimpses of eternity are given to mortals who, even if we are not made of mud, have a very close relationship with the earth on which we stand. In or around AD 524 Boethius was clubbed to death after allegations of treason, a fact not entirely unlike other facts about the history of humankind and not entirely easy to reconcile with his words about eternity. Brains capable of experiencing 'the complete and perfect possession of unlimited life all at once', even if only for a few seconds, can be destroyed in a few seconds. Being in time and space, needing our bodies with their brains, we cannot see beyond these moments when we glimpse eternity and we cannot even be sure that they are genuinely revealing glimpses. So is it a real possibility that we who are 'flesh' are capable not only of glimpsing, but also of entering, and sharing, a reality which is at least as far beyond us as the life of freedom is beyond the prisoner who looks at it through a window with bars?

To answer that question with a 'Yes' or 'No' or a 'Don't know' is to make a personal decision which will seem mistaken to those whose personalities are different, often because they have been profoundly influenced by different cultures. And this difference seems to have something to do with the contrast between the two hemispheres which are the most recently evolved parts of the human forebrain. Neuroscience has demonstrated that in the right hemisphere dwell most of our powers of intuition, imagination and passion: there we make patterns, harmonies and desires and there we 'believe'. In the left hemisphere are most of our powers for the acquisition and analysis of factual information. There we 'think': we reject illusions, we formulate reasonable and accurate language dealing with facts, and we apply this kind of knowledge to many achievements through practical skills. Fortunately it is normal for the two hemispheres to be connected physically, and to do each other's work up to a point, but the disunity of the human brain may account for some of the disagreement between 'soft' and 'hard' responses to mysteries which may or may not half-hide great realities. So without being able to prove anything in response to the mystery of death, I must try to offer a vision (not mine alone, of course) which comes, I hope, through both hemispheres but which may cause offence either to the right or to the left.

The 'singularity' in the energy which was the first version of matter, or whatever else was the unimaginable event from which the universe evolved, can be called 'creation' in a spirit of great awe. Science does not include words such as 'purpose' (still less does it speak of 'design') but religion has to try to answer the question: why does anything exist at all, rather than nothing? To religion, it can seem to be a real possibility that the Creator's purpose is indicated best when we use the word 'love'. Developing that insight, it can appear that our effort to understand 'eternity' should not exclude either what is (by analogy with our own emotions) the 'sorrow' of the Creator when Boethius is deprived of life within time and space, or the 'joy' of the Creator that Boethius can be given a share in eternal life. God, it seems, is changeless in the sense that he does not change or suffer or rejoice as we change or suffer or rejoice. He is himself, the 'I AM' encountered by Moses in the desert, the God who is reliable despite the tragedies later experienced by Israel, by Jesus and by humankind.

But what is changeless and reliable can, it seems, be enriched and it appears that the divine intention of being enriched goes some way to explain why anything exists – and also why the Source of existence permits existence to be imperfect, even tragic. What merely exists must be less perfect than God, and God has chosen to give what exists some independence – which can go wrong. But God is able to make the best of things. In his fine academic exploration of the difficult idea of *The Creative Suffering of God* (1988), Paul Fiddes suggested that 'we might think of God's eternity not as an abolition of time but as a healing of it. At every moment of his divine life he would be integrating the flow of the past, present and future into a new wholeness, redeeming the past and anticipating the future in a new harmony.' That is an example of mythological or metaphysical language, but it seems less misleading than many other examples.

A clue to this mystery seems to be provided by the word 'character', which may be less open to misunderstanding than the word 'soul'. It is a word which indicates what is essential in a reality which in its fullness may be extremely complicated. The full reality of God cannot be simple. In the Bible there is a profusion of images about God; in the creation there is a very large mass of facts which point in different directions, or in no stable direction at all, if we ask what was the purpose in giving them existence; and, at least in its older books, the Bible includes images of a cruel God which correspond with the facts which leave on us the painful impression that Nature is not nice. But when taken as a whole, the message of the Bible is that 'God is Love': that is what all the images boil down to, God's character. Similarly, many human beings, and perhaps all, are complicated. What we know about ourselves tells us that no simple words of praise or blame could tell the whole truth. And we find that other people, even people we know very well, are often unpredictable. Yet we feel able to speak about a person's 'character'. From the depths of our own personality, as known (however dimly) when we look into a mirror of self-analysis, a character emerges which, as we recognize, is also known to others, however partially. We spend much of our time thinking and talking about the characters of other people.

It seems that any real possibility of life after death for humans depends on God being, in his own eternal life, directly the basis of the characters or souls which are the essences of personalities. Before death these characters or souls depended on, and were shaped by, their bodies and their physical and social environment. In every particle of their existence it mattered to them that they were girls or boys, women or men, healthy or handicapped, genetically influenced to be happy or not, or clever or not, and socially developed by their experiences of family and neighbourhood, education and culture, marriage or singleness, class and work. When they die, all of that history dies, 'earth to earth, ashes to ashes, dust to dust'. Many pictures have been painted, in art or words, of 'resurrected' and 'glorified' bodies. These are all the work of human imaginations. But because they are not photographs of the dead it does not follow that they have no significance. They are images which are signs, signalling that the people whom God loves for ever, and to whom he gives life for ever, are people who have been shaped by the world which is also his creation. Now they depend on their Creator alone.

There lives the one realistic hope of surviving death and of being given an eternal life which is infinitely more than survival. As a great Anglican archbishop, William Temple, put it in *Nature, Man and God* (1935), 'Man is not immortal by nature or as of right, but he is capable of immortality and there is offered to him resurrection from the dead and life eternal if he will receive it from God and on God's terms'. And the great Protestant theologian Karl Barth spoke of 'unconditional participation in the glory of God'. Like many others in the history of religious thought I have found it helpful to compare this kind of resurrection by God with remembrance by God. This seems to be in keeping with the prophet's insight that God's memory is stronger than a mother's memory that she has a child (Isaiah 49:14, 15) and with the cry of the dying bandit in Luke's gospel (23:42): 'Jesus, remember me when you are a king!' Of course this comparison is inadequate, for the divine 'memory' cannot be like a powerless mourner's memory of days gone by, but perhaps it is a little like a lover's memory which by its action makes the remembered past glorious. If God is both parent-like and supremely powerful, he will want to make the best of 'me'. If Jesus is 'King', the 'me' who is remembered in eternity is not a mere continuation of the 'me' who died beside him; nor is the 'me' extinguished. Human memory can be creative and less cannot be true about the 'memory' of the Creator. As he 'remembers', God creates – and creates a life far, far better because from first to last his motive is love.

What Jesus reveals, supremely as he dies, is that the love which most people know as the greatest fact in their lives is, on an infinitely larger scale, the greatest fact about God. It seems strange that the modern search for evidence about life after death has concentrated on the possibility or impossibility of communications from the dead, when what most people actually affirm when confronted by death is the enduring significance of their everyday experience of love. People who do not think that there can be any kind of life after death can still defy death by keeping memories alive and by making them precious. Others who grieve can refuse to think that the one who is loved has been annihilated. The experience of loving has been the most important thing in their lives and although they may be inarticulate about this they may have an intuition that here they have touched the deepest level of reality and glimpsed something more real than death itself. It takes two to make a friendship and a friend may protest against the idea that death has ended a friendship for ever. A widow may ask 'Shall I see him again?' and not think that question silly. Of course people are not blind to the facts about death but in countless printed announcements or carved monuments, and even more in thoughts which are private and heartfelt, love denies that death kills everything. Let us take and use this as the key to the door which separates us from what comes after death, from what is eternal.

It is natural for many people who grieve to long to be in touch with the dead. It is also natural, and right, for people who believe that the dead (particularly the dead whom they love or admire) are in some senses alive, to cling to a hope – the hope that the dead care about them and their struggles and needs. But if it is the case that the best key to this mystery of death is provided by God's love to which our own loves are introductions, it seems to follow that the best way of thinking about the dead is to think of God's love for them, to the best of our ability – which may be small during our grief. That is prayer for them – not prayer which may suggest that God needs to be influenced by us if he is to love the dead, but prayer which does what it can to rise into awareness of the love which God already has, before and after death. It also seems to follow that the best way of believing that the dead care about us is to believe that they share God's own love for us. That is prayer by them for us – not prayer which may suggest that the saints are nicer, or more interested, than God, but prayer which relies completely on the divine love which could not be closer to us than it already is. And so it seems best to pray to God and not to the dead, although it is understandable that many people have prayed to saints – who presumably pass on the messages to the only possible source of existence and of good.

This is not a book in which there is space to repeat the experience, observation and thinking which have fed the religious tradition which I have accepted as the nearest approximation to the ultimate truth which is available to me. In this space it may be enough if, after asking for such forgiveness as is needed for being personal, I say that the alternative to belief in the Creator (who is of course much more than personal) is a belief that from the Big Bang (or whatever else) onwards, through those vital first three minutes, the entire universe is ultimately an immense series of accidents – a belief which (together with the vast majority of humanity) I find incredible. The alternative to the belief that the Creator has done something to explain himself is the belief that he is not truly God because he does not deserve to be worshipped by the humanity he has left in total darkness – a belief which is incompatible with the conviction which arises from all religious experience that we encounter a reality superior, not inferior, to our own consciences. The alternative to the belief that the Creator is extremely patient because he sets an extremely high value on his creation's freedom is the belief that he is already in complete control of what goes on – another belief which I find incredible, because from our viewpoint as we observe evolution, history and our own experience, much of what goes on does not suggest that it is controlled by a God both very loving and very powerful. And the alternative to believing that the best revelation of God is to be found in what Jesus Christ taught, did, was and is, must be (I believe) finding a better revelation. I have not found one. What I have found is that Jesus reveals that God has a purpose which he wants us to understand, a purpose which involves both the acceptance of much freedom in his creation and a determination not to be finally defeated by evil. The prayer of Jesus was 'Your kingdom come!'

Can this faith answer some old questions?

7

Are Souls Immortal?

THE BELIEF IN 'RESURRECTION' involves a belief that a person can be raised to a share in the eternal life of God – and raised by an act of God. That implies that the personal identity which may be called the 'soul' can survive the body's death, but it is different from the belief that the human soul is immortal, meaning that it is incapable of dying whatever happens to it and whatever may be its character. This belief in the 'immortality of the soul' has often been linked with the idea of 'pre-existence', the belief that the soul had the same identity before the body which is now attached to it was conceived and born. It has often also been linked with the idea of 'reincarnation', the belief that when its present body dies the soul will be inserted into another body unless it already deserves entry into the final bliss.

A classic exposition of the immortality of the soul, carrying with it those two other ideas, is found in Plato's *Phaedo*, a reconstruction of the conversation between Socrates and some of his friends before his execution in 399 BC. This dialogue has never lost its attractiveness. As Phaedo, who is presented as the narrator, says about Socrates:

> he died so fearlessly, and his words and bearing were so noble and gracious, that to me he appeared blessed. I thought that in going to the other world he could not be without a divine call . . . What astonished me was, first, the gentle and pleasant and approving manner in which he received the words of the young men, and then his quick sense of the wound which had been inflicted by one of their arguments, and the readiness with which he healed it.

But the Socrates of this dialogue is not merely a philosopher who teaches patiently: he is a brave man who has resisted the temptation to escape death. He could have won the court over by withdrawing the teaching 'against the gods' which brought about his sentence to death by poison, and since the sentence was questionable he could have gone into exile after offering a bribe. He now offers poetic visions to make his beliefs about life after death vivid and, more eloquently still, he is a shining example of spirituality and morality. He is as certain about the reality of the gods 'as I can be of such matters'; he regards himself as the 'consecrated servant' of Apollo the god of light; his last words before dying ask for a little sacrifice to the god of healing; his first contribution to the dialogue is to say that since the gods are 'guardians' who 'care' about the lives they have given to mortals, suicide is wrong; and he often speaks about 'God' in the singular. His last command to his disciples is to 'take care of yourselves', by which he means to 'despise anything more than nature needs' and to dedicate life to the search for absolute justice and truth, beauty and goodness. He is convinced that this search will be rewarded after his death and therefore he is glad to die.

But Plato's *Phaedo* has also been found useful as a text which may be analysed critically as an introduction to philosophy, since many of its arguments can be shown to be invalid. The student can be challenged to spot the defects and to try to do better.

One question which critics ask concerns the character of the dialogue. Plato, although a disciple of Socrates, was absent from this final conversation because of illness. His reconstruction of what his master taught on this occasion is difficult to reconcile with his account in an earlier book (the *Apology*) of the defence which Socrates had made at his trial. According to that account, Socrates said then that death might mean extinction and that God alone knew whether or not it did. Had he spoken to the jury then as he was represented in *Phaedo* as speaking to his disciples, it would have been impossible to convict him on the charge of atheism. So what did Socrates really think? Indeed, what did Plato think? In *Phaedo* he did not speak for himself, and in other books he used other arguments and other myths, often revising the teachings which emerged from his earlier writings.

Here Plato's Socrates produces arguments which can be demolished quite easily, sometimes by Plato himself in later work. He maintains that the soul (*psyche*) is not mere 'breath' (the original meaning of the Greek word) but belongs to the same category as the eternal 'idea' or 'form' (*eidos*) of equality or beauty. So his ability to persuade us that souls are immortal depends on convincing us that these 'ideas' which souls know are eternal. He insists that the soul existed before the conception of the body – but he does not explain how, in that case, it was the soul of a human being. He claims that some forms of intellectual ability (elsewhere he uses as an example a slave boy's ability to understand geometry) derive from knowledge of the 'idea' or 'forms' before birth – but he cannot claim that any particular piece of knowledge does not need to be learned. He is eloquent about the glories of the eternal life which the soul knew and can know again – but he cannot explain what is the point in being born into this world of imperfection. And the basic suggestion, which is that what the dead know is more real than what they knew on earth (elsewhere he uses the image of moving into the sunlight from the darkness of a cave), can be criticized. In *Survival and Disembodied Existence* (1970) Terence Penelhum made the point that if God is not the great reality known after death, all that can be claimed is 'that the imagining or dreaming or hallucinating is, in default of there being objects in an environment to perceive, all that survivors can do'. This objection could be countered by saying that the 'ideas' known by the dead, such as perfect beauty and justice, are identical with the reality of God, and that the existence of the dead depends on the existence of God; but this is not what Plato says. When he is at his most deeply religious the 'idea' (or 'form') of 'the Good' is the object of his worship. In some sense, 'the Good' seems to cause what is good on earth but this relationship is much vaguer than what is meant when it is said (by others) that 'God' creates all that exists; when considering that concept, Plato uses a variety of myths, the chief one being that the Demiurge fashioned the world from existing matter, using the eternal ideas, specially the Good, as he struggled with this material.

It is claimed in *Phaedo* that the soul 'rules' and 'despises' the body and is therefore more than the body's 'harmony', but this claim has often been contradicted by appealing to common human experience. It is a fact that sometimes we make decisions on spiritual or moral grounds which are not to our physical advantage, but in reality our personalities are not split unless we are suffering from a mental disease, and it is often healthy and wise for what we call our 'soul' to listen to the wishes of the body. The soul – whatever that may be – is very firmly embodied before the very great crisis of the body's death.

Plato's whole approach in *Phaedo* and elsewhere has justly been called elitist: when he says that only 'philosophers' can hope for rapid access to heaven (as he does more than once) he uses that word in its original meaning, 'lovers of wisdom', but in practice he shows little respect for non-intellectuals, and no willingness to think seriously about their prospects. Sometimes he seems not far from the theory of his great pupil Aristotle that only the power of pure reasoning survives death, although in his *Republic* he expands the soul to include an element of 'desire'. In *Phaedo* his theory about life after death involves the belief that souls which have been 'stained' by too close an association with their bodies are sent back to the earth as animals or birds of prey. Even people who have 'practised the civil and social virtues without philosophy' may return in suitable reincarnations as bees, wasps or ants. In this dialogue the possibility that non-philosophers may not exist at all after dying is not explored, but we may be forgiven if we reckon that our extinction is more likely than our reincarnation as ants.

Near the end of Plato's *Republic* Glaucon is asked by Socrates: 'Are you not aware that a human soul is immortal and imperishable?' The immediate reply is a look of astonishment on Glaucon's stupid face. But most of the disciples of Socrates seem to have been quicker to agree. They were privileged young men, excited by the growth of their mental powers, and they were prepared to add pre-existence before conception and reincarnation after death to the very old tradition that death is somehow survived.

Burial sites which seem to be about 30,000 years old show that when a hunter-gatherer, *Homo sapiens*, knew how to use stone tools and fire, but not yet bronze or iron, some (at least) of the dead of this species were buried with care, which is not the systematic practice of any other species. Neanderthal Man, who developed by a route parallel with the road taken by *Homo sapiens*, did the same. Seeds found in some very ancient sites suggest that flowers or foliage could be used and the bones of animals may show that meals near the grave were thought to be somehow shared with the dead. Implements and ornaments, presumably for use after death, were buried. Red ochre could be painted on bones when the flesh had decayed, or put in graves, and appears to indicate a belief that life would return by resurrection. The alignment of some of these bones on an east–west axis may indicate a comparison between the human journey through death with the setting and rising of the sun. Whether or not there was any such thought, it seems almost certain that there was some belief in some part of the life of the dead human somehow continuing in order that the whole person could somehow, some day, enter a new life. This belief would connect, although in a way we cannot understand, with the blend of religion and magic which inspired the paintings which survive on the walls of caves.

There is of course no direct evidence of such beliefs before the invention of writing (by which date they were widespread) but almost all non-modern people observed by modern travellers and anthropologists maintain a tradition that human death is survived by some sort of a spirit. Sir James Frazer, a very secular-minded anthropologist who wrote three large volumes on *The Belief in Immortality and the Worship of the Dead* (1913–24), reached this conclusion about 'savages' and made it a ground for his fascinated disapproval of human thought before the rise of science. His summary was that 'among savage races a life after death is not a matter of speculation and conjecture, of hope and fear; it is a practical certainty which the individual as little dreams of doubting as he doubts the reality of his own existence'. More recently, visitors have discovered non-modern individuals who do doubt the truth of what their societies corporately take for granted, for many non-moderns are able to think in a very down-to-earth fashion. Anthropologists have therefore modified Frazer's assumption that to be 'savage' is to be stupid. They have also stressed that the dominant belief in survival should not be regarded as always wishful thinking: on the contrary, life after death was usually thought to be either very inferior or else positively dangerous to those who were fully alive. Very ancient burial sites can show that the body was bound, with the knees drawn up towards the chin, and some non-modern peoples continue that practice. It can be interpreted as suggesting that the body is asleep or awaits a new birth; but the usual explanation, by non-modern peoples and those who study them, is that the dead are believed to be able to harm the living unless they are kept firmly in their places. Stones heaped above a corpse may be intended either to protect it or to imprison it.

This life of the 'shade' or 'spirit' or 'soul' after the death of the body was generally accepted as a fact by the Greeks who were the ancestors of modernity. It was not necessarily a pleasing fact. Some 800 years BC, Homer's *Odyssey* included (at least in the version which we have) the story of how the shade of the dead hero Achilles was able to speak because he had been given a sheep's blood to drink. He then declared that he would prefer to be the slave of the poorest peasant alive in Greece rather than be the king of the land where he half-survived among 'the mindless dead, images of the mortals who have been overcome'. To Homer's imagination dead heroes could take some comfort from hearing about the deeds of their descendants, and the imaginative power of later poets (Hesiod and Pindar) sent the spirits of semi-divine heroes to the Isles of the Blessed in the ocean to the west, where the sun set. When it was known that the earth was round, a still later generation could send the blessed to live above the stars.

Sculptures on tombstones surviving from Athens at the height of its glory depict a sadness which is still poignant as the living take leave of the dead who depart to an unknown destination. Inscriptions often say *chairé*, which can mean 'be happy' or simply 'farewell'. They give no sign of a belief that the immortality of the soul involves pre-existence before conception and reincarnation after death. Through the survival of these tombs and other evidence we know what beliefs were commonly held. Great importance was attached to a decent burial with frequent visits to the family's graves, sometimes leaving food behind. (In the play by Euripides, Antigone is regarded as a heroine because she sacrificed her own life in order to sprinkle dust on her brother's corpse.) There were hopes of family reunions, and on regular public holidays the spirits of the dead were invited to return to the places they had known. The general picture is of a belief in survival but not in the glorious immortality which is the monopoly of the gods – and even the possibility of survival can be questioned by a few sceptics. In *The Bacchae* Euripides asked whether perhaps all religion was mad and in *The Frogs* Aristophanes mocked the discussion about the afterlife: would it be in meadows or in mud?

Not surprisingly there was considerable interest in the possibilities that more might be known about life after death and that what might be known could be good. 'Mystery' religions offered initiations into cults around myths of dying and rising divinities usually linked with the death and resurrection of the natural world in autumn and spring. Athenians and others processed each autumn to Eleusis where some were initiated, it seems by the display, in a candlelit celebration, of symbols representing the revival of

Persephone in the cult of her mother Demeter, a goddess of fertility. The cult of Dionysus, also a fertility god, brought its devotees (mainly women) to ecstasy at night by the use of alcohol, drugs and dance. The cult of the dying-and-rising Orpheus almost certainly influenced Plato although he disapproved of the emotionalism stirred up by the priests. An Orphic passport could be inserted into tombs, with a formula to be recited: 'I am a child of earth and the starry heavens; I am dry with thirst and I perish but give me quickly the cool water which flows from the Lake of Memory.' This was in contrast with a myth used by Plato, that in the land of the dead, souls had to drink from the Lake of Forgetting – which explained why they did not remember their many incarnations.

However, if the ideas of pre-existence before conception and of reincarnation after death were not at the centre of the religion of Ancient Greece, they have been prominent in the religions of Asia and of a remarkable number of places, including those continents which used not to be in communication with Asia.

Various theories not involving any divine revelation have been advanced about how these beliefs began and became so widespread. It seems likely that there is some truth in most of them. We are all conscious that we have inherited a lot from the past, and the question of exactly what we have inherited remains mysterious even after the discoveries of genetics and of child psychology. Sometimes the skills of young people (for example, in music) amaze us and we may ask whether these skills were not learned before the present life began. Sometimes we may ask more sadly whether the handicaps with which some children are born result from misdeeds in a previous life. Sometimes we ourselves have the strange feeling that some experience of ours is only a repetition of what happened at a time we cannot remember. And sometimes animals seem remarkably like people, perhaps like people who lived before these animals were born.

As we have noted, the objection is raised by modern people, including philosophers, that the person now alive (or the animal) cannot be the same as the person who lived in an earlier generation, and it is a fact of history that the classic expositions of the beliefs in existence before conception and reincarnation after death seldom included any claim that the details of another life could be remembered. However, there were some such claims and in modern times more have been recorded, chiefly by the American investigator Ian

Stevenson and also in India and other countries. Some of these claims have been falsified by discoveries that during the present life a book or document was read, or a film or TV programme was viewed, which suggested the relevant 'facts' – although the 'memories' claimed were not necessarily fraudulent since the actual memories may have been half-buried. Other claims have been met with the kind of suspicion which has been a response to the claims of parapsychology. But such criticism has been heard mainly in the West and in those parts of the rest of the world which have been heavily influenced by the science developed in the West. And even in the West, public opinion polls have shown that in recent years many people have accepted pre-existence and reincarnation. Some polls have suggested that such believers may amount to a tenth or even a quarter of the population. They cheerfully ignore the argument that their belief is nonsense since they cannot have existed before they were conceived by their parents.

The strength of these beliefs in the vast population of Asia is shown by the rating of the *Bhagavad Gita* (the Song of the Blessed One) as the greatest of the Hindu scriptures, assembling in a poem of great beauty all the most important ideas in India's religious history. The Gita has also impressed many in the West since its first translation in 1785. Its anonymous author composed it between 300 and 200 BC, not very much later than the writing of another imaginary dialogue, *Phaedo*.

In the oldest Indian scriptures, the hymns called the Vedas, there is little evidence of an interest in life after death, assumed to be a shadow of the life which these Aryans lived to the full. Interest quickened in the period of the Upanishads, sacred books written over a long period, perhaps 800–300 BC, and then it took the form of a belief in pre-existence and reincarnation. The soul (*atman*, which like *psyche* or *pneuma* in Greek originally meant 'breath') is essentially eternal, uncreated and free from change, but it can experience life on earth in one after another of a large number of bodies which need not be human. Which class of body is allocated to the soul is decided not by the judgement of God, or of a god, but by the automatic operation of a law of cause and effect: the better the actions (*karma*) in one body, the better the prospects of life in another body, for souls can enter wombs which are 'pleasant' or 'stinking'. Since every reincarnation involves some suffering, however, the supreme purpose of religion becomes the 'liberation' (*moksha*) of the soul from the earthly lives which constitute 'wandering' (*samsara*).

India's religious teachers have envisaged different ways in which a soul is connected with *Brahman*, the eternal 'being, consciousness and bliss' behind all the named gods and all the universe; and the contents of the wisdom attainable by self-discipline and meditation have also been somewhat different.

One form of the Hindu tradition is extremely different from (for example) the faith of Ancient Israel. Here *Brahman* and *atman*, the divine and the human, are essentially one. In the famous story, a young man's eyes are opened wide by the shock of the words: 'That art thou!' To those who adopt this position which can be expounded in philosophy as 'monism', the presence or absence of a body is basically insignificant, for everything conditioned by space, time or causation is *maya* (usually translated as 'illusion'). But there is a second position, 'dualism'. It can be taught that souls and all the other components of the universe are the 'body' of Brahman with some difference between them and It. Or it can be taught that the soul is more definitely dependent on Brahman, in life or death. These positions are associated with the philosophers Sankara, Ramanuja and Madhva, who worked long after the writing of the Gita. Both monism and dualism can inspire *yoga* ('union'), which prepares for union with the divine by physical and spiritual exercises, but dualism can be linked with *bakhti*, the humble devotion to God perceived as a person and as saviour. In *bakhti* the embodied soul comes closer to the God who is 'beyond the All' and 'beyond the beyond': 'He is Another'.

All these themes come together, although with no precise definition, in the poetry of the Gita. Lust, wrath and greed are the gates into darkness (16:21) but the soul can be detached from the passions like a tortoise withdrawing its limbs into its shell; the soul can still be like a lamp which does not flicker in a room which is closed to every wind; and then the soul can flow into Brahman as a river flows into the ocean. 'Beyond this creation, visible and invisible, there is the invisible, exalted Eternal' (8:20) – and it can be reached. All this can be learned and done by a form of *yoga* which may include the traditional prayers and sacrifices but which reaches higher. It asks for no favours in return but simply adores, offering worship, work and the rest of life as a sacrifice which needs to be reduced to ashes in unselfish and trustful faith and love. Such *yoga* imitates the unselfishness of God himself, whose loving activity is ceaseless whether or not it is acknowledged. And such *yoga* has its reward, in the vision of God and in union with God. This 'Song of the Lord' has its climax in an overwhelming revelation of the wonders of the creation, 'the body of the God of gods' (11:13), but supremely in the wonder that Brahman can say 'you are dear to me' (18:61–66).

However, like Plato's *Phaedo*, the Gita may be criticized. It is a myth which tells of the appearance of Krishna as a reincarnation of Vishnu, one of the three ancient chief gods (along with Brahma and Shiva). He has volunteered to drive the chariot of Arjuna, a prince who although his cause is just has been unwilling to fight against his kinsmen in a civil war (the main subject of the *Mahabharata*, the vast epic in which this *Gita* is included). Krishna persuades him to fight and, if need be, to die or to kill. The main consolation which he offers is not that Arjuna is on the right side in the war. It is that those who will be killed have already been condemned to die physically because of their bad *karma* (11:33), but in spiritual reality neither the slain nor the slayer can die, for 'we have lived for all time: I and you and those kings of men . . . The Eternal in Man cannot kill: the Eternal in Man cannot die'. Therefore the wise 'do not grieve for those who live or for those who die' (2:11–19). If Arjuna or anyone else should be killed in battle, it will be no more than if he were to change his clothes (2:22).

Fighting, with an acceptance of its consequences, is Arjuna's duty (*dharma*) since he has been born into the caste of the warriors. 'To die doing one's duty is life' just as 'to live doing another's duty is death' (3:35). 'No work stains a man who is pure' (5:7) provided that he does this duty in a spirit which is 'at peace in pleasure and pain, in gain and loss, in victory and defeat' (2:38) because the mind is fixed 'beyond what is done and not done' (3:18). And if any stain should reach the soul of Arjuna as a result of doing his duty as a warrior, he can be assured by Krishna that 'he who at the end of his time leaves his body thinking of me comes unto me' (8:5). 'He who loves me shall not perish' (9:31), but shall enter *Brahman*, the ultimate and divine peace (2:72); in *Brahman* the soul shall find 'everlasting joy' (5:21). Those who worship other gods or ancestors or lesser spirits 'go to them' (9:25) only to be sent back to earth in a new body and so 'return to the cycles of life in death' (9:3). The person who 'strives and fails' to be good before death 'dwells for innumerable years in the heaven of those who did good' before being sent back to earth, 'carrying with him the wisdom of his former life'. He is 'born again in the house of the good and the great' (6:41–43). The person who has not even tried to accumulate good *karma* suffers a worse fate.

Some criticisms of the Gita which have been made in the West (amid much praise) seem to be unfair. It does not encourage idleness: 'not by refraining from action does a man attain freedom from action' (3:56). Rather, the person is praised 'whose work is made pure in the fire of wisdom' (4:19). The teaching is that it is right to do one's duty by working but it is wise not to expect too much from one's work: so it is shrewdly observed that job satisfaction almost always ends in tears. Nor does the Gita encourage aggression: in the civil war in which Arjuna is involved, he is summoned to defend what is said to be justice. Nor does it encourage superstition. The *yoga* which it does encourage is far more than the magical recital of Krishna's name: naming him as Saviour is only the climax of a *yoga* which, according to temperament and circumstances, can take the form of 'resting the heart' in devotion but also of concentrating the mind, of consecrating work or of humility with good will for all (12:2–14). This spiritual masterpiece therefore supplies plenty of material to feed the prayers of saints and non-violent revolutionaries such as Gandhi and to inspire commentaries such as the one by Sarvepalli Rhadakrishnan, the scholarly President of India who deserved the international respect in which he was held.

Nevertheless, in its original setting the Gita did use religious language to command the acceptance of duties within the social system of India established by the Aryan conquerors, who after a time seem to have used the existing belief in reincarnation held by the conquered people as a support for this system based on conquest. The work which was now praised did include fighting and killing in a battle which was more than the battle of the soul against spiritual evil; this battle is said to have lasted for eighteen days. The social system which was now blessed did divide society into the priests who offered sacrifices, the rich and the powerful who were the patrons of the priests, the less privileged but still respectable who fitted into the system, and the outcastes whose human rights were violated every day. The Gita asserted that this division into castes 'came from' Krishna himself (4:13). It also offered absolution to any whose consciences were troubled by participation in violence or injustice and not quietened by the sacrifices in the temples: their immortality would be union with the glory of Brahman if they died with their thoughts fixed on Krishna. In the Gita, Krishna is an incarnation of the ultimate reality to which the English word 'God' refers, but with all due respect for Indian religion it can be said that it is not accidental that the setting of this scripture is a battlefield, for long before he was revered as an incarnation of God Krishna was first known to recorded history as himself a warrior, the chief of the Yadava clan.

The Hindu reply would of course be that this point made by a Westerner is insensitive to the true glory of the scripture. The same reply could be made to Western questions about the Gita which are more philosophical. Nevertheless, such questions have been raised. How can Arjuna be sure that he existed before his present life if he has entirely forgotten that earlier existence? How can he be sure that he deserves to be privileged if he does not know how or when he earned it? And how can he be sure about the power of Krishna as Saviour if the ultimate power has hitherto lain with the inflexible system of *karma*?

The most effective protest against elements in the Hindu tradition has, however, come from within India – and its influence has been vast as it has protested against previously dominant religious traditions in other Asian countries and, in modern times, against the materialism of the West.

Gautama Siddartha, the *Buddha* (the Awakened One), died probably towards the end of the fifth century BC, perhaps 80 years before Socrates. Although his early years had been sheltered in a palace he was dismayed by what he saw outside and defined his mission: 'There remain birth, old age, death, sorrow, lamentation, misery, grief and despair. I am prescribing for their extinction in this present life.' His teaching would extinguish these evils by extinguishing desire and attachment more thoroughly than the Gita advocated (although the Gita was influenced by Buddhism). The Buddha rejected both the sacrificial system and the social system which the sacrificing priests asked the gods to bless. He urged those who would listen to work out their own salvation without relying on any priests and he welcomed into his community of disciples or monks men and women from any social group. He did not accept the necessity of a great cycle of reincarnations, although stories were to be told of his own previous 550 lives. That repetition can be ended by ending the complex of perceptions, thoughts and desires called the 'soul' or the 'self'. There is no need to face another life of suffering. The continuing identity of this complex can be 'blown out' like an extinguished candle in *Nirvana*, when it 'cannot be apprehended' any further. The best form of compassion for suffering humanity is to spread the knowledge of these truths, to open the path to this kind of enlightenment.

In the Buddhist tradition, therefore, immortality is not an idea which may be supremely attractive but which is contradicted by our knowledge that we need our bodies in order to exist. Immortality is a fact, a truth which every sensible person takes for granted, but it is also an extremely unpleasant fact from which every sensible person must struggle to escape. The ending of the cruder forms of selfishness, and after that the ending of the distinguishable identity of the self, are the supreme, but very difficult, tasks of human life. In comparison with that task, any question about the existence or non-existence of gods or Brahman is unimportant. So is any question about the existence or non-existence of a person between death and rebirth. Asking about such matters was, the Buddha said, as foolish as not being willing to remove a poisoned arrow until the victim could be told who shot it.

The earliest Buddhist texts (in the 'three baskets' of the Pali canon) suggest that death and reincarnation follow each other without interruption unless the desirable obliteration of the self has been achieved before or while dying. However, as Buddhism spread to the north and developed, it became clear that it had retained or revived elements in the Hindu tradition which the Buddha himself had rejected. Particularly in Tibet, China and Japan, many Buddhists in the tradition of the *Mahayana* ('Great Vehicle') have hoped for heaven, have feared hell and have prayed for guidance and aid to many gods and goddesses, to Bodhisattvas (the 'enlightened' humans who have postponed Buddhahood in order to teach others) and to the Buddha himself. It could also now be believed that the complex of perceptions, thoughts and desires can hold together after the body's death sufficiently well to remain conscious and active, defying the force (the 'fierce wind') of *karma* and achieving Nirvana by reliance on instruction and help received from this tradition. The complex can be addressed as 'you'.

A guide to dying and the afterlife used in Tibet since the fourteenth century AD has been well known in the West since its translation into English in 1927 as *The Tibetan Book of the Dead*. The language and ideas are, however, so difficult to translate that the English version could still puzzle readers when it was revised. The book is said to have been written four centuries before its frequent use began and clearly it is a compilation of traditions known and obeyed for many years, including much Indian mythology. It has not been used throughout Tibet, and there are rival books, but it has been acknowledged as representing widespread beliefs. It seems more appropriate for use by an elite than by the common people; its instruction is often addressed to one who was 'nobly born' and it takes for granted the presence by the deathbed of helpers who are able both to read and to understand complicated religious beliefs. On the other hand, 'if the deceased is of the common folk, say "Meditate on the Great Compassionate Lord"', and this simple person-to-person contemplative prayer is said to lead to a recognition of the truth about the *Bar do* (the state between death and Nirvana or reincarnation).

This *Bar do thos grol* was intended for reading to the dying and the reading was to continue for a considerable period after death, close to an ear, before the corpse was buried or cremated after a delay for this purpose of at least three days. Later the reading would be continued in a place familiar to the deceased.

It is thought wise to invoke in prayer the help of many named divinities, and the compassion of the Buddha is believed to be able to 'pull and push' a self towards Nirvana. But the Buddha himself and many Bodhisattvas, gods and goddesses and lesser spirits who seem to surround the path of the dead must be known to be, in reality, mere 'ambushes'. They must be seen as 'reflections of my own consciousness, my own thought forms'. The dead person is told: 'these are radiances shining from your own intellectual faculties. They have not come from any other place. Do not be attracted by them. Do not be weak or terrified. Remain in a state of non-thought-formation.'

To begin to think about 'suchness' is to lose all possibility of entering Nirvana, which demands that the consciousness should be 'undifferentiated' like water joining water. The only image of Nirvana which is useful is the extremely bright and clear light which shines on the newly dead, perhaps 'for about the time a meal takes' or perhaps 'for a snap of the fingers'. Unless concentration on this Brightness without figures or colour is maintained, the dead person will see visions of peaceful and pleasing, or wrathful and terrifying, divinities in colour. These represent not supernatural reality but the reviving and enslaving human passions. There may be visits to heaven or hell, also imaginary. All these experiences take up to 49 days. Finally the dead person, if unwilling to be purified for Nirvana but not destined to become an animal, will imagine a human couple enjoying sex. If the deceased is more interested in the man, the soul will enter a womb and be born as a girl; if in the woman, as a boy. In either case the soul would be doomed to live and die, the penalty for being fascinated by life.

The book insists that all experiences after death are imaginary apart from the vision of Nirvana and it may be asked why it has impressed not only Tibetans but also many people (one was the psychologist Carl Jung) who have studied it in places very far from its earthly setting – and in places where thought seeks 'suchness' or precision instead of avoiding it. The bright light may well be derived from near-death experiences and the visions of peaceful or wrathful divinities from the near-death review of happy or shameful memories. The choice against Nirvana may well be the choice for a return to life when near death. The teaching that life begins in sex is not mysterious. But some of the interest taken in the claim to describe life after death in detail seems to have arisen not only from a natural curiosity but also from the elitism which has been noticed in *Phaedo* and the Gita. Here the privileged, who have the best chance to become an *urhat* passing straight from death to Nirvana, are not philosophers or warriors: they are the monks and their friends who have access to this book of instructions. Ordinary humans can only be advised to meditate on the compassion of the Buddha, although in history that teacher refused to say more than that the effects of behaviour before death usually, and sadly, set in motion a process which led to the presence of this complex of perceptions, thoughts and desires in yet another body.

The development of the Buddhist tradition in Tibet and elsewhere seems therefore to be a radical departure from the teaching of the tradition's founder. Such developments are not unknown in other religions. This one, however, may be understood sympathetically as an attempt to recover a belief even more widespread than Buddhism: the belief that there is a reality which may be called 'you' or the 'soul' or the 'self' and that it survives the body's death. Moreover, this development of Buddhism agrees with many other religious traditions that this reality not only survives, but also develops after death. The soul of a Tibetan would have a continuing history of development if it was sufficiently conscious as an individual to be able to decide between the rival attractions of Nirvana or peaceful and wrathful divinities, and to choose whether to be male or female before reincarnation.

When the Tibetan Buddhist tradition is related to modern needs and questions, its strength can be shown, as in Christine Longaker's *Facing Death and Finding Hope* (1998). The author, who dedicated her life to helping to meet the emotional needs of the dying and the bereaved after the painful and very distressing death of her husband, offers much advice which many other pastors and counsellors would recognize as wisdom which does not depend on any particular religious or philosophical belief. She urges the carer to be 'free of myself', giving 'unconditional love'. She hopes that the person dying will be told the truth unless the situation is exceptional; that what can be done will be done to heal poisoned memories and broken relationships; and that so far as is possible any pains and anxieties which cannot be controlled otherwise will be treated with detachment, viewing these troubles as someone who is maturely wise watches children playing noisily. Whether or not we can agree with this Buddhist's verdict that 'our present existence is one of continuous suffering', we can admire this advice about deathbeds. It must be true that the end of our present existence can be eased if there can be a spiritual conquest of the attachment which grasps and refuses to let go. With King Lear, I have to learn how to 'endure' my 'going hence' as I once endured my 'coming hither'.

So her book is unquestionably wise about facing death. But what hope is to be found?

Her central message is a modern version of Tibetan Buddhism and is that the 'innermost essence' of a person is different from the 'troublesome ego'. Our essence is utterly peaceful, while the ego is turbulent with materialistic thoughts and selfish emotions. The hope must lie in the belief that after death 'you do not exist' unless the ego or 'personal soul' is so worldly that it is dragged back by its 'habits' into another existence in the world, another 'false identity' for the 'innermost essence'. What is desirable is the true absorption of the 'innermost essence' into 'emptiness', as when the space inside a vase is enabled to join the space outside by the shattering of the vase.

In her book this union with emptiness can be called 'being with God'. It is taught that throughout one's life it is important to establish a personal relationship with, and trust in, God; and acts of devotion to God, Christ or the Virgin Mary are praised as helpful to the dying. But it is made clear that 'God' does not exist in anything like the sense in which mainstream Christians believe in God, and it is hard to see how this 'God' deserves trust and devotion. The emptiness which is here called 'God' may give a meaning to our existence somewhat as the horizon gives shape to a view of the countryside, but this 'God' is neither substantial nor permanent nor powerful any more than the horizon is. This 'God' seems close to the 'Nature' which is more familiar to the West and which also does not in any real sense care for, or preserve, the life of any individual. Christine Longaker's teaching is wise in many ways about the difficult business of dying, and is compassionate towards those who die or grieve, including those who trust in God, but in the last analysis her message does not seem to be essentially different from the crudely blunt saying that 'when you're dead you're dead', and her avoidance of that clear conclusion seems to arise out of her courtesy.

It may not be too discourteous to Christine Longaker, and to the many who hope to die with the attitude which she advocates, if a further question is raised briefly. In such teaching about death, is there a healthy attitude to life? As a result of his explorations in the half-hidden emotional lives of his patients, Sigmund Freud suggested that a 'death instinct' is a part of humanity. By that he did not mean merely the truism that since all life dies 'the aim of all life is death'. He meant that the prospect of death can be welcomed, and self-destruction may actually be chosen, because it is our 'pleasure' to return to the womb, before the rise of the selfhood which separates and creates anxiety. Freud himself was fascinated by death, all his life. He had a habit of saying to his friend and biographer Ernest Jones, at the end of a meeting, 'You may never see me again.' But having this dark fear, he rejected the 'death instinct' in favour of life, of honest and courageous individuality, of rational coping with reality, and he tried to help his patients to make the same choice. We need not believe all his theories but this understanding of mental health as a preference for the 'life instinct' despite its penalties seems correct, and it may be combined healthily with a belief (which he reckoned to be an illusion) that the undying God is so substantial, permanent and powerful that he can raise the personal identity of humans above their deaths, unless they themselves choose death.

But, in reality, does a human being include any element capable of surviving and (it may be) developing after the body's death? Or to ask the stronger question: is the soul incapable of dying?

To many modern people the answer to all questions about possibilities of survival after death is so obviously 'No' that no discussion is thought necessary. These people may, however, be attracted to other elements in the Buddhist tradition, so that it is accepted and recommended to others as a method of attaining freedom from materialism, greed, lust, hatred and anxiety within the boundaries set by extinction at death. In a contribution to a book of essays on *Death and the Afterlife* (1989), Francis Cook, a professor at the University of California, recommended a Buddhist attitude to life but argued that any doctrine of reincarnation is a 'convenient fiction'. It is convenient 'because it serves as a powerful inducement to live the kind of moral life that is prerequisite to liberation'. The new form of Buddhist teaching is brutally clear that death brings the end of all perceptions and desires; after it nothing endures or changes because nothing exists. That is what we must perceive to be the truth, and even what we must desire since the annihilation which always comes at death is Everyman's automatic Nirvana; and when we accept it, we shall find ourselves liberated and at peace. This truth demands not only that we should be less selfish but also that we should admit that we are not our 'selves'. We are mere assemblies of impulses and fears, images and ideas, which on the whole make us unhappy. Therefore we should have no regrets as we move towards their total destruction by death.

To Professor Cook this seems to be the only legitimate conclusion to be drawn from modern knowledge of the physical basis of personality. This, he thinks, is what survives from Buddhist teachings, ancient or modern – teachings which (more than any other religious tradition) deserve to be treated with sympathy and respect. This is what is true for him when Plato (for example) insists on the nobility of human life by mistakenly claiming that the human soul is naturally immortal. But Cook's conclusion may not be correct.

8

Are Bodies Raised?

MANY GENERATIONS OF CHRISTIANS were taught to believe in the 'resurrection of the flesh' and although the Nicene Creed affirmed only the 'resurrection of the dead' the expectation about 'flesh' was included in the so-called Apostles' Creed in the original Latin. In the sixteenth century the Book of Common Prayer began to make the translation 'the resurrection of the body' familiar in the English-speaking world and in the nineteenth and twentieth centuries this phrasing of the hope began to be interpreted by many Christian teachers as 'the resurrection of the personality. This meant that after death the personality or 'soul' willing to share the life of God will be provided by God with whatever spiritual reality is needed in order to maintain the personal identity which, before death, was given by the body of flesh and bones, together with all the physical and social environment of that body. It has seemed sensible not to take the Apostles' Creed more literally at this point. At other points too that ancient creed, originating in a summary of the teaching given to candidates for baptism in Rome, used pictures of physical events to convey spiritual truths, and it is now generally agreed that (for example) 'he ascended into heaven and is seated at the right hand of the Father' are not the kind of events that could be filmed for the news on television.

The difficulty of taking the 'resurrection of the body' more physically can be illustrated from a book with many strengths, first published in 1976: *Death and Eternal Life* by John Hick, a philosopher who is a courageous and constructive advocate of dialogues between religion and modern thought and between the world's religions.

Hick interpreted the 'soul' as 'a valuing name for the self', accepting from science the truth that 'the self has been gradually formed by the interaction of a partly random selection of genetic information with a particular historical environment'. 'In the course of this interaction', he added, 'an element of freedom, or creativity, is exercised.' But less wisely he allowed himself to be led into speculations about the resurrection of the body. His motive was entirely honourable: the desire to reinterpret the ancient belief in reincarnation in a way that might make sense to modern people. He suggested that the old belief about souls being added to new bodies in this world was a mythological expression of the truth that souls are given new bodies in other worlds. He wrote about the possibility of 'the divine creation in another space of an exact psycho-physical "replica" of the deceased person'. 'Resurrected persons', he added later, 'would presumably be able to identify each other in the same kinds of ways and with a like degree of assurance as we do now.' But these suggestions seem no less mythological than the beliefs of the past and many questions have been asked about his suggestions. Can we talk meaningfully about 'another space' of which we have no knowledge? What does 'psycho-physical' mean if the new body is neither spiritual nor physical in a sense we can understand? And can a person's identity be preserved by the creation after death of what is only a replica? Even if I were to be able to shake hands, could I be sure that this really is my old friend? It may seem that Hick anticipated the force of these questions, for in his book he said plainly that he did not believe that this resurrection of the body will be the final state. There will be 'a series of lives, each bounded by something analogous to birth and death, lived in other worlds'. The final, heavenly state will lie 'beyond separate ego-existence', when 'it may be that embodiment is no longer necessary'.

Another exposition of the idea of the resurrection of the body has come from an equally impressive Christian thinker, the Cambridge physicist John Polkinghorne. In *Belief in God in an Age of Science* (1998) he maintained that 'Christian hope of a destiny beyond death is expressed in terms of God's resurrection act of reconstituting us in our bodily identity in the environment of the new creation.' He stressed that the new creation will be new: 'the "matter" of the world to come, which will be the carrier of this re-embodiment, will be the transformed matter of the present universe, itself redeemed by God beyond its cosmic death'. His expertise in the advanced study of physics enabled him to draw some support for this belief from the possibility of imagining universes consisting of matter very different from the material of the universe which scientists have begun to explore. But it can be questioned whether any kind of scientific knowledge is relevant to the belief which this distinguished scientist holds, for the 'matter' which scientists investigate is, he says, to be 'redeemed' by being 'transformed' and the question remains whether, in that case, it should rightly be called matter. And it may also be asked whether this belief holds out a really convincing and consoling 'Christian hope of a destiny beyond death', for it contrasts strongly with the idea that a penitent bandit could be with the dying Jesus 'today in Paradise' (Luke 23:43). It suggests that our resurrection may have to be delayed for tens of thousands of millions of years, until the history of the universe has been completed.

Another recent interpretation of the resurrection of the body has been offered by Keith Ward, the Regius Professor of Divinity in Oxford University. In *God, Faith and the New Millennium* (1998) and elsewhere he, like Dr Polkinghorne, has provided a persuasive restatement of Christian beliefs which takes full account of the findings of the natural sciences about the evolution of the universe and of humankind on this planet. But when he turns to the future he, too, has allowed himself to be in danger of leaving the impression that Christian faith in life after death involves the kind of fantasy which entertains us in science fiction. That cannot be his intention.

He of course accepts that 'the law of entropy decrees that, in the very long run, all physical energy in this universe will run out into darkness and inactivity' but he teaches that Christians hope for a 'new creation' bringing 'transformed embodiment in a world beyond this physical cosmos'. He warns us that 'such transfiguration cannot occur until the last freely choosing human being has been born, and until the present laws of nature, which entail suffering to some degree, are changed', but he suggests that meanwhile there will be 'afterlife worlds' which he calls Paradise and Sheol, the latter being a condition of sufferings which are 'real and grievous'. These pains are 'caused by our own actions' but they bring repentance and purification. Both 'afterlife worlds' are temporary and therefore they seem to involve special kinds of space and time. It is also hoped that there will be great progress within the space and time which we know, ending in the 'transformation of this cosmos, by means of the self-directing understanding it has generated, into new forms of embodiment, expressing the life of the Spirit more fully and creatively than is possible in a universe doomed to eventual decay'. Some exciting ideas about the future of humankind on this planet are included in this connection but it is made clear that these are guesswork. There may be a disaster as big as the collision of a comet or meteor with this planet (such a past event seems to have resulted in the extinction of most species then alive, including the dinosaurs) but other possibilities include 'some form of genetic engineering that will enable humans to evolve into higher forms of life', or the making of machines which will be 'artificially constructed personal beings', or the advantages to be derived from 'contact with alien beings from some other solar system'.

It is understandable why Ward teaches that 'the Christian faith is above all a hope for the setting free of creation from its bondage, to allow the divine purpose to come to its full fruition', for he can refer to St Paul: 'the creation waits with eager longing for the revealing of the children of God' (Romans 8:19). However, if we are looking for what 'the Christian faith is above all' to people who accept modern science's assurance that ultimately the universe including this planet must decay and collapse, it seems more realistic to prefer Ward's own statement that 'every achievement in knowledge, art and virtue is co-operatively caused by the Spirit and remains forever in God's unforgetful being'. Since as Ward says 'it is fairly clear that any enduring goal for the cosmos must lie beyond this physical space-time', it is also fairly clear that talk about the goal in terms drawn from physical space-time uses (in his words) 'highly symbolic imagery': it is not matter-of-fact talk. The great fact is God who, Christians believe, has declared his will to make other spirits eternal. As Ward puts it himself, 'God wills to unite all souls to divinity.'

Much as Professor Hick had the entirely honourable intention to reinterpret the Eastern belief in reincarnation to modern people, so Professors Polkinghorne and Ward wish to interpret to the age of science the biblical pictures of judgement and glory at the end of the present age of the world. But in the time when the Bible was written the rise of modern science lay in the distant future, the end of this age, or of this world, was expected, or at least hoped for, in the near future, and the new age 'to come' was of course imagined in images taken from the culture known to the writers. Thinking out the relevance of these biblical pictures to scientific knowledge is evidently no easy task.

So critical questions can be asked about belief in the resurrection of the body as involving physicality, however mysteriously. More critical still are the questions likely to arise in response to the belief in its old form, where the transformation of matter received much less emphasis. And the history of this belief began long before the birth of Christianity.

As we noted, during many centuries *Homo sapiens* appears to have hoped for the resurrection of the body buried in a simple grave. Some flesh buried in the dry sands of Egypt has been preserved across 5,000 years. Paradoxically, it was the addition of the honour of coffins that put an end to this natural preservation of corpses. It was the later addition of golden ornaments and charms, and very expensive furniture and sculptures in elaborate tombs, that made it inevitable that grave robbers should damage the embalmed body which was encased in the 'mummy'. This working-class crime was punished very severely but it was the practice of some pharaohs and noblemen to throw out their predecessors' bodies for the sake of economy as they took over their tombs. According to Ancient Egyptian beliefs any damage to the embalmed body was a spiritual calamity, for a soul called the *ka* was supposed to dwell in the corpse or, failing that, in an adjacent statue. Magical rites were performed over it, actual or symbolic food was fed to it and many of the paintings on the walls were intended to represent meals or the preparation of food. Another surviving soul, the *ba*, also spent most of its time in the body although it was free to wander and to give messages to the living. If the body was destroyed the *ka* and *ba* would cease to exist, a belief which was held to justify the enormous expenditure of resources and skills on the construction of tombs and on ever more elaborate embalming. It must have been very difficult for the Ancient Egyptians to accept that all this effort was in vain (the desperate priests of Thebes, the modern Luxor, collected royal mummies and hid them in two undecorated cellars) but eventually it had to be acknowledged by others that if a soul required a body in the afterlife a supernatural miracle would also be needed, beyond the reach of any human embalmer or magician.

Many Christians have expected such a miracle from God. 'The resurrection of the dead' in the Nicene Creed has been held by Eastern Orthodox teachers (most notably by Gregory of Nyssa) to involve a resurrection which is physical in a sense which has not been sharply defined but which is in practice not distant from the 'resurrection of the flesh' in the Apostles' Creed (whose authority has not been denied in the East although it has been used more in the West). Only in 1513 did the Fifth Lateran Council of the Catholic Church in the West make the 'immortality of the soul' a necessary belief and even then it was little more than a preliminary to the 'resurrection of the body' in connection with the Last Judgement. Belief in a physical resurrection, more straightforwardly physical than anything taught by St Paul, is recommended by an improbable story which has found its way into the New Testament, that 'the graves opened and many of God's saints were raised from sleep, and coming out of their graves after his resurrection they entered Jerusalem, where many saw them' (Matthew 27:51–53). Belief in the resurrection of the flesh is found clearly stated in the second century (the oldest surviving Christian treatise on the resurrection of the dead, attributed to Athenagoras of Athens, affirms it although some passages are more Pauline) but we may briefly refer to the two leading teachers of the Church in North Africa.

Tertullian, who died around AD 225, was not impressed by Plato's teaching about the immortality of the soul. Socrates, he said, was the 'worst of teachers', possessed by a devil and determined to restrict admission to heaven to philosophers who shared his own sinful love for young men. The idea that the soul is inhaled when the newborn infant draws breath is wrong: to be sure, 'the soul is the temporary inhabitant of the flesh', but it is lodged by God in the flesh at the moment of conception. The idea of reincarnation is also mistaken: to be sure, Hades is 'a vast deep space in the interior of the world', but there 'every soul is detained in safe keeping until the day of the Lord' when it will be reunited with its own body.

Tertullian was not embarrassed by the teaching of Jesus that the dead will live 'like angels' and of St Paul that 'flesh and blood cannot inherit the Kingdom of God'. He explained that Jesus meant that the saints will be equal with the angels and that St Paul meant only that our present flesh will be changed while being resurrected. Flesh is, he was sure, necessary. Even the soul, he believed, was composed of very fine material particles transmitted by the father. Since Adam was created miraculously out of earth, at the end of time people's bodies will be re-created appropriately, and such a miracle is to be expected in view of the fact that every spring, life is raised from death in Nature. In the Old Testament the resurrection of the flesh was (he claimed) predicted by Ezekiel's vision of the dry bones being given life and clothed with flesh (in chapter 37) and by the story of Jonah being released from the belly of the whale (although both the prophetic vision and the miniature novel are now thought by almost all scholars to have been intended by their authors as parables promising new life for the people of Ancient Israel after being conquered by their enemies). But Tertullian's argument also depended on considerations about what seemed to be justice. Our flesh deserves resurrection because it was created by God the Father and fully shared by God the Son. Our behaviour while in our flesh may have been good, in which case the flesh deserves to be rewarded for its part in the good life, or evil, in which case the flesh deserves to be punished for luring us to sin.

The whole idea of flesh being resurrected at the Last Judgement seemed strange, indeed obviously mad, to many of his contemporaries, but Tertullian was prepared to answer awkward questions. 'What will be the use of the entire body when the entire body will become useless?' Answer: indeed the flesh will not have any of its old uses, but 'the judgement seat of God requires that Man shall be kept entire'. Will the resurrected bodies be subject to passions? Answer: they will be perfect, restored with all their equipment, but because food, drink, sex and work will no longer be needed there will be no more hunger, thirst, lust or weariness. If the flesh will be rewarded by resurrection, what is the point of denying it food by fasting? Answer: lighter bodies will rise more quickly to heaven and the slim will find it easier to get through heaven's gates. Will the resurrected bodies perpetuate damage sustained before or during death? Answer: 'we are restored to what is natural, not to what is injured'.

Augustine, who died in 430, was deeply influenced by Platonism but as his theology developed he insisted that 'all who are Christians must confidently believe that there will be a resurrection of the flesh at the coming of Christ to judge both the living and the dead'. He now agreed with many of Tertullian's points and also attempted to answer questions. Where is the soul located at present? Answer: throughout the body. What will be the age of resurrected bodies? Answer: around 30, the best age and the one at which Christ rose from the dead. If these bodies are in heaven and heaven is above the sky, will they not fall to earth? Answer: they will be weightless. Will all the hair they ever grew grow again, since Christ promised that not a hair on the head of a saint will be lost? Answer: they will have enough hair to avoid any imperfection. What will become of human flesh eaten by a cannibal? Answer: it will be separated from the cannibal's flesh. Will the scars of a martyr's wounds disappear from the perfect body? Answer: they will remain as badges of honour.

Both these theologians were trying to think out a convincing way in which people now very much embodied could be given eternal life. They attempted to answer this serious question in a world where the contrast was deep between the emphasis of philosophers and religious teachers on the immortality of the soul, with a contempt for the world of ordinary humanity, and the absorption of most people in the crude materialism of daily life. How could Christianity affirm the enduring value of the spiritual without denying the importance of the physical? Teachers such as Tertullian and the greater Augustine helped the Church to win the battle against the Gnostics ('people in the know') who were hostile to the flesh and to the rest of the material creation. In his *Early Christian Creeds* (1950) J. N. D. Kelly summed up the early history: 'Quite understandably, in view of their opponents' caustic jibes about the materiality of the flesh as such, the champions of orthodoxy made it a point of honour to use the word with all its realistic associations' and 'this vigorous, full-blooded realism set the pattern for later orthodox thought on the subject'.

Not only did Ignatius, the prisoner and martyr, say that when he was resurrected his chains would be like strings of pearls: another martyred bishop, Cyprian, warned women who used face powder that God himself might not be able to recognize them when they came to be judged. Not only did the mother of the first Christian emperor (Constantine) discover three crosses still buried in Jerusalem; she also learned which was the cross of Jesus when one was said to be able to raise the dead physically. Far more influentially, by the year 700 the 'assumption' of the mother of Jesus into heaven, soul and body, was being celebrated in the Western as well as the Eastern regions of the Church: historians have traced the belief back to Palestine in the fourth century, although it may be older. Since then countless Christians have rejoiced that Mary received this privilege and they have had this image in their minds as they have thought and prayed about their own survival of death. And while no physical relics of Mary could be venerated, the cult of the bones of the saints became a massive ingredient in the religion of the Dark and Middle Ages. Gold, jewels and prayers surrounded these relics (whether authentic or not) and one reason was the belief that one day, perhaps soon, they would rejoin other bones in the glorified bodies of the resurrected saints, so that devout and perhaps miserable people still alive could feel near to their prospect of glory. Under such powerful influences and with encouragement from the leaders and thinkers of the Church, the imaginations of Christians, fed by the development of representational art, especially in Western Europe, became increasingly materialistic.

The teaching of the greatest of the theologians before Augustine, Origen, envisaged the bodies of the resurrected as being 'ethereal, of shining light' – but his treatise on the resurrection was lost, probably because it was not approved, and his disbelief in a physical resurrection was denounced fiercely by prestigious teachers of the Church such as Jerome. The teaching of the greatest of the medieval theologians, Thomas Aquinas, was that resurrected bodies would be supernatural, with a new 'clarity' and 'agility' as well as with a new freedom from passions and weight: they would not be a mere reassembly of particles once buried. Yet the Lateran Council of 1215 required the belief that 'all will rise with their own individual bodies, that is the bodies which they now wear'. Aquinas himself was clear that 'if the body of the man who rises is not to be composed of the flesh and bones which now compose it, the man who rises will not be the same man numerically'. He was so sure that the soul was no more than the 'form' (Aristotle's term) of the body that he taught that while awaiting the resurrection of the body the soul is not truly a person. Increasingly, people took an interest in reports of saints' bodies being made ready for heaven by not corrupting in their graves; and a very great poet, Dante, imagined souls in heaven as having 'aerial' bodies before they are reclothed with flesh at the resurrection. Souls in purgatory also have bodies made of air, but so made that they are capable of feeling pain. Even Aquinas could agree that the tortures in purgatory and hell are physical in a very terrible way, and could explain that the perpetual gnashing of teeth will not damage the supernatural enamel.

Modern knowledge has added questions which might have defeated even theologians of that stature. Is it meaningful to call a thing 'flesh' which will not be subject to the natural law which decrees that, in everything physical, 'entropy' (disorderliness in the constituent particles) will sooner or later end that thing's existence? If we are to be resurrected in 'flesh', where will all the humans ever born be housed (plus all the embryos in naturally or artificially terminated pregnancies)? Will the whole universe be adjusted so that we can be comfortably accommodated on a sufficient number of habitable planets? And so forth. It can be argued that theologians such as Tertullian, Augustine and Aquinas were right to insist on the resurrection of the flesh whatever may be the difficulties, since this is an essential part of the tradition based on the Bible. But there we shall find very little of the dogmatic certainty which has been characteristic of much of the official teaching of the churches. In the Hebrew Bible which is called by Christians the Old Testament, the difficulty of believing in any kind of desirable life after death is acknowledged so completely that the belief is very slow to arise as a part of the common faith of Jews. In the New Testament this belief is given a central position, mainly because it was so strongly believed that Jesus had been raised from the dead and had appeared to the apostles, but still it is said very often that faith is needed if this is to be believed – and it is not said at all precisely what will be the nature of 'resurrection' for us, or what was the nature of the body in which the risen Jesus 'appeared'. According to the New Testament, resurrection is a reality but the details are hidden from us.

Let us therefore open the Bible again.

During most of its history Ancient Israel had no thought which has been recorded that life after death could be desirable, except as a release from the worst miseries of life before death. In the Hebrew Bible the word *sheol* ('no-land') usually refers to the grave, and prayers to be delivered from it are prayers to be saved from death. Psalm 88 is a prayer for deliverance by someone 'on the threshold of the grave':

> I am numbered with those who go down to the Abyss
> and have become like a man beyond help,
> like a man who lies dead
> or the slain who sleep in the grave
> whom you remember no more
> because they are cut off from your care.

And Psalm 146:4 is equally negative:

> Man breathes his last breath,
> he returns to the dust:
> that is the end of all his thoughts.

A 'wise woman' reminds King David that 'we shall all die: we shall all be like water spilt on the ground and lost' (2 Samuel 14:14) and this despair explains the famous intensity of the king's grief for the death of his rebellious son Absalom. When another son dies, David's certainty that he will 'go to him' is a cry of resignation, not of hope (2 Samuel 12:15–23). It is no consolation to think that a half-life persists. The story of the occasion when David's predecessor as king, who is already doomed, uses a medium to summon the grumpy prophet Samuel up from *sheol* (1 Samuel 28:3–20) teaches that nothing but gloom is derived from contacts with the dead, for which the penalty prescribed by the religious law is death (Leviticus 20:27). Ghosts merely 'squeak and gibber' (Isaiah 8:19). The contrast with other peoples who revered, consulted and fed the dead is great. But equally significant is the absence from the teaching of Israel's prophets of any clear word that obedience or disobedience to Yahweh (God) will be rewarded or punished after death. Instead, all are equal and all are weak in the land of the dead. The Book of Isaiah, for example, does not threaten the king of Babylon, who is 'the oppressor', with the tortures of hell. Instead it imagines 'all who have been kings of the nations' taunting him because now in *sheol* 'you have become weak as we are', as he lies on a bed of maggots with worms for a covering (14:3–11).

The prophet Hosea (6:2) speaks not of resurrection after death but of the recovery of Israel as a people on earth, when

> after two days he will revive us,
> on the third day he will restore us,
> that in his presence we may live.

And it is on Mount Zion, a hill in the city of Jerusalem, that 'the Lord will prepare a banquet of rich fare', 'will swallow up death for ever' and 'will wipe away the tears from every face' – which is almost certainly an extravagantly rhetorical idea that after the promised recovery of the people no one will die (Isaiah 25:6–8). It is less clear what is promised in a poetic passage of lament and hope for Israel whose climax is Isaiah 26:19:

> Your dead will live, their bodies will rise again,
> those who sleep in the earth will awake and shout for joy,
> for your dew is a dew of sparkling light
> and the earth will bring people long dead to birth again.

But King Hezekiah is clear that the dead cannot praise Yahweh (38:19) and the last words of the Book of Isaiah, which have inspired many visions of a hell in eternity, were intended to convey a vision of a new Jerusalem in a new world. The rubbish dump of this city will resemble Gehenna, suggested by the Valley of Hinnom outside the old city, and there may be seen

> the dead bodies of those who have rebelled against me;
> their worm shall not die nor their fire be quenched,
> and they shall be abhorred by all.

At the end of Psalm 17 there is a hope of a vision of God after awakening, but this seems to be after a night's sleep, not after death. In Psalm 73 there is glimpse of 'glory' in 'heaven' but the main theme is that Yahweh will guide the faithful on earth and save them from 'death with all its terrors'. Less ambiguous is the dawn of a belief that Yahweh is Lord even of the *sheol* described in the Book of Job (10:22) as 'the land of gloom and chaos where the light comes as darkness'. Psalm 139 is a prayer, although it draws no specific conclusions from its trust in the Lord:

> Where can I escape from your spirit?
>   Where can I flee from your presence?
> If I climb up to heaven, you are there;
>   if I make my bed in the grave, there also I find you.
> If I say 'surely the darkness will cover me
>   and night will close around me',
> darkness is not dark to you
>   but the night shines like the day
>   and to you dark and light are one.

Searches of the Scriptures discovered passages which could be interpreted as meaning that a very few heroes of Israel who had trusted in the Lord had been 'assumed' (caught up) into a heaven located above the earth without having to die. Such were Enoch, who at the age of 365 'was no more because God took him' (Genesis 5:24) and Elijah who ascended in a whirlwind on a chariot of fire (2 Kings 2:11). It could be believed that Moses had been 'assumed' since his grave was unmarked (Deuteronomy 34:6).

However, a strong conviction about Yahweh's treatment of the dead did not emerge until the end of political independence had brought a new interest in the life of the individual, in the difference between the righteous and the wicked and in the vindication of the righteous in the 'age to come'. It is usually agreed that this development was influenced by the Zoroastrian religion in Persia. Although the details are not clear in the hymns attributed to Zoroaster himself, the prophet's followers believed that on the fourth day after death the soul is judged. Good souls enter light, bad souls will fall into darkness from a bridge which becomes to them as narrow as a razor's edge, and a cosmic battle is fought between the Creator (Ahura Mazda) and the Spirit of Evil (Ahriman). Finally, in accordance with beliefs held by many, a Saviour descended from Zoroaster but born miraculously will raise the bodies of the dead and cause them to enter Paradise (a Persian word for a great garden).

In the middle of the second century BC Jews faithful to their religious traditions were being persecuted, not rewarded as their prophets had promised: they were being punished by a ruler determined to modernize the country in accordance with the fashionable Greek ideas. Not surprisingly, their intensified hopes about the 'age to come' now combined solid rewards for the righteous with terrible punishments for the wicked. A Jew who was being tortured was said to have uttered with his last breath: 'The king of the universe will raise us up to a life made new.' A mother of martyrs encouraged her sons: 'The Creator . . . will give you back life and breath again, since now you put his laws above all thought of self' (2 Maccabees 7:1–23). A little later, sacrifices were offered in Jerusalem with the prayer that there would be forgiveness for Jews who had died in battle with pagan charms hidden under their tunics. This novelty was explained as having in view 'the wonderful reward promised to those who die a godly death' (12:39–45). The Book of Daniel seems to have been written in about 165 BC as propaganda for this rebellion, and at 12:2 it interpreted the promises and threats of the Book of Isaiah as meaning future rewards and punishments for individuals on earth:

> Many who sleep in the dust of the earth will wake,
> some to everlasting life
> and some to shame and everlasting abhorrence.

But the book immediately went on to express a belief surprisingly like Plato's notion of philosophers in heaven:

> The wise leaders shall shine like the bright vault of heaven,
> and those who have led the people in the right path
> shall be like the stars for ever and ever.

When the persecution of Judaism died down temporarily, there remained the oppression of the pious poor and fresh anger provided fuel for the detailed imaginations of a considerable series of 'apocalyptic' (revelatory) writers. There could be predictions of 'great torment', not merely destruction, for the wicked in Sheol, which had become a capacious underworld full of life, however unpleasant. But the main emphasis was on rewards for the remnant of the faithful and the righteous.

The Eighteen Benedictions formulated not long before the birth of Jesus for regular use in synagogues praised God because 'you bring the dead to life'. It seems that most Jews believed this although the Sadducees, conservative aristocrats some of whom ran the Jerusalem Temple, correctly pointed out that this belief was not taught in the older and more sacred parts of what became the Hebrew Bible. Although they hated the Sadducees, the Essenes seem to have taken little interest in any question about life after death: their Dead Sea Scrolls, discovered in the 1940s, show that their enthusiasm was reserved for the coming of the end of this evil age on earth, when the Jerusalem Temple would be purified. The Pharisees formed the largest religious movement and the Jewish historian Josephus recorded that they 'believe that souls have power to survive death and that there are rewards and punishments under the earth for those who lead lives of virtue and vice'. 'The souls of good alone pass into another body' while 'eternal imprisonment is the lot of evil souls'. It is clear from other evidence that the Pharisees believed in a single resurrection rather than many reincarnations, but Mark's gospel (8:28) says that Jesus was thought by the people to be 'John the Baptist' or 'Elijah'. Almost certainly that is not a reference to a belief in reincarnation in the Indian style. It seems to refer to an opinion that much as 'the spirit of Elijah rests on Elisha' (2 Kings 2:15), so Jesus carries on the prophetic mission of Elijah and the Baptist. But there may also be a reference to the popular belief that Elijah, who had been carried into heaven instead of dying, would return to earth, and we are told that thoughts could be so confused that both 'Herod' and 'people' could believe that Jesus was his contemporary John the Baptist, 'raised from the dead' (Mark 6:14–16). Josephus himself seems to have had ideas close to the philosophy of Plato as well as to Zoroastrian religion. He wrote that he believed that those 'who depart this life in accordance with the law of nature and repay the loan which they received from God' have spotless souls which are 'allotted the highest place in heaven' before they return to earth to find new homes in new bodies. And there were other Jews who clearly believed in the immortality of the soul more or less in the style of Plato or in the popular version of that style. This belief was taught in some of the 'apocalyptic' books of the time, but also in a book which was included in the Greek translation of the Hebrew Bible, although not in that Bible itself.

Its author lived in the cosmopolitan Egyptian city of Alexandria a hundred years before the birth of Jesus of Nazareth but adopted the polite fiction that he was King Solomon. He wrote in Greek and found the Greek idea of the immortality of the soul more acceptable than the belief that 'by mere chance we were born and after our lives we shall be as though we had never been; for the breath in our nostrils is but a wisp of smoke; our reason is a mere spark kept alive by the beating of our hearts and when that stops our body will turn to ashes and the breath of our life will disperse like empty air' (2:2, 3). Such scepticism may be found within the Bible (Ecclesiastes 3:9–21).

The reply was not that a physical resurrection awaited faithful Jews. It was that already

> the souls of the righteous are in the hand of God . . . They have a sure hope of immortality and after a little chastisement they will receive great good, for God tested them and found them worthy to be his. Like gold in the furnace he put them to the proof, and

> found them acceptable like a sacrifice burned whole on the altar. When God comes to them their ashes will kindle into flame . . . They are his chosen and grace and mercy shall be theirs. But the ungodly shall meet with the punishment which their evil thoughts deserve . . .

And the author made other affirmations. Without mentioning the story of Adam and Eve, he claimed that death was not an essential part of human nature and destiny. 'God created Man for incorruption and made him the image of his own eternal self, but the devil's spite brought death into the world and death is reserved for those who take his side' (Wisdom of Solomon 2:23–24). Even before death, now 'a perishable body weighs down the soul' (9:15).

To sum up: there was a considerable diversity of beliefs among the contemporaries of Jesus. A glorious future could be imagined, physical or spiritual, in the sky or on earth, in all the world or in the land of Israel, in the restored Garden of Eden or in eternity. Jerusalem would be at the centre, a 'new' Jerusalem – but how new was not agreed. The images used to express these beliefs or visions had to be physical and were probably not meant to be taken literally. There was often inconsistency within a single book. About the hope for life after the individual's death, the cool words of E. P. Sanders in *Judaism: Practice and Belief 63* BCE*–66* CE (1992) seem to be wise: 'we are left knowing that Jews – certainly a lot, probably most – believed in an afterlife and in individual reward and punishment' while 'at some times some people indulged in detailed fantasies about the other world'.

After the massacres accompanying the failures of the Jewish rebellions against Rome, the reconstructed community was led more firmly by the Pharisees and taught more systematically by the rabbis. As earthly hopes faded, the hope of the miracle of physical resurrection for faithful Jews was at the centre but more spiritual and wider hopes were not forgotten. It was believed that punishment after death would be 'for all generations' if the sins were of the mind, but it could also be taught that sins of the body would be chastised for twelve months only. At least one medieval rabbi, Joseph Abo, maintained that the suffering in hell would be no more than a perpetually frustrated longing for physical pleasures, while the Kabbalah movement taught that the souls of people not yet ready for the 'Garden of Eden' or Paradise would be educated by a series of incarnations in different bodies. It is again difficult to know precisely what most Jews believed: the family's mourning during the week after a burial was intense but no funeral service has survived which was written down before the ninth century of the era shared by Jews with Christians.

The greatest of all Jewish theologians, Moses Maimonedes who died in the year 1204 of this era, concentrated on the immortality of the soul. He was accused of advocating the immortality of philosophers but actually he taught that eternity was the ultimate destiny of all Jews apart from those guilty of specially serious and unrepented sins, who would be 'cut off' or destroyed rather than punished by tortures. The 'saints of the nations of the world' would be included in this destiny. Most of the medieval rabbis did not differ from Maimonedes in holding out hope for the righteous Gentiles but he was attacked for denying the resurrection of the flesh and late in life had to defend his orthodoxy by writing a treatise accepting that belief. The physical resurrection, however, would occur only during the temporary kingdom of the Messiah on earth. The Messiah and all those resurrected would have to undergo bodily death before entering the true glory, spiritual immortality.

Beginning with Spinoza in the seventeenth century there was a fresh stirring in Jewish thought and those who were prepared to revise the traditional rabbinic doctrines began to say openly that their belief was in the immortality of the soul. These liberals included Hermann Cohen in his Jewish version of the 'enlightened' philosophy of Immanuel Kant, and Moses Mendelssohn in his version of the philosophy of Plato. When Jewish modernism was organized in the USA as 'Reform', its manifesto, the Pittsburgh Platform of 1885, explicitly renounced belief in the resurrection of the flesh. Jewish Orthodoxy has maintained that traditional belief but the Jewish theologians best known to Gentiles have almost all agreed with Reform in this particular. It also seems fair to say that even the immortality of the soul has not been greatly emphasized. In the agonized discussion of possible religious responses to the Holocaust in the 1940s, the consolation of a strong belief in heaven has not been prominent. Some Jewish teachers have concentrated on the resurrection of the state of Israel, also in the 1940s, thus returning to the position taken in most of the history of Ancient Israel, but many modern Jews have become more or less secularized and there is an active debate about the question: what can be the identity of Judaism without faith in the God who brings the dead to life?

In the Jewish movement which became Christianity there were, as was to be expected, beliefs very close to those of all the other Jewish movements apart from the Sadducees. (The idea that Christians need not believe in any form of immortality or resurrection did not find much expression before the twentieth century AD.) But the original form of Christian belief in life after death has been oversimplified in order to be either attacked or applauded. On the one hand, the mental world of the early Christians has been said to be mythological or fantastic, like the Greek myths about dying-and-rising, autumn-and-spring, divinities or the Jews' own fantasies about a coming golden age. This criticism deserves to be taken seriously because it seems certain that there were mythological or legendary elements in what the early Christians said about life after death, including their Lord's life. On the other hand, the New Testament has been applauded for giving evidence which no intelligent and impartial person would wish to refute about a physical resurrection which actually occurred in down-to-earth history, namely the resurrection of Jesus of Nazareth: his tomb was undeniably empty, his resurrected body was seen eating and was heard speaking. This position also deserves to be taken seriously, for it seems certain that a momentous event did take place in Palestine in the spring of AD 30 or 33. The surviving evidence is, however, not simple.

St Paul was thoroughly a Jew and what survives of his teaching about life after death has elements which match the various strands of Jewish belief. The oldest surviving Christian document, from around AD 51, records what he taught converts who had been pagans 'serving idols' in Thessaloniki, where an inscription on a tomb has also survived. It preserves one pagan's despair: 'Marathonis laid Nicopolis in this tomb, wetting the marble with his tears, but it brought him no profit. What is left is only sorrow for a man alone in the world without his wife.' Paul gave the church in Thessaloniki a word-picture which adapted current Jewish beliefs. The Book of Daniel had included a vision of 'one like a man' (representing the saints of Israel, it seems) 'coming with the clouds of heaven' to the Ancient in Years (7:13). Now these Christians were to 'wait expectantly for the appearance from heaven' of Jesus the

Son of God, 'whom God raised from the dead' (1 Thessalonians 1:10). Until that appearance, the dead 'sleep in death' (4:13).'At the sound of the archangel's voice and God's trumpet-call . . . first the Christian dead will rise, then we who are left alive will join them, caught up in the clouds to meet the dead in the air. Thus shall we always be with the Lord' (4:16–18).

The other surviving letters of Paul do not include a systematic theology or any intention to provide one. Instead he taught in the Jewish style, by assembling images without thoroughly explaining them and without making them completely consistent. In this case it is difficult to think that he believed that God would literally blow a trumpet and it is impossible to know exactly what he believed would become of the Christian dead, previously 'asleep', after they had met Jesus in the air. When he returned to the subject in his first letter to Corinth (chapter 15) he still hoped to be alive when Jesus returned to earth and in other ways he showed himself to be a man of his time. He accepted the strange custom of being baptized 'on behalf of the dead' which the Mormons were to revive in the nineteenth century. He believed that Adam's sin brought death to humanity (as stated more fully in Romans 5:14, 15), that a seed dies in the earth, that humans and beasts do not have the same evolving flesh, and that the brightness of the moon is not derived from the sun. But as he attempted to 'unfold a mystery' and speak about resurrection for the living and the dead, he rose above many of his contemporaries and successors.

He taught that the body (*soma*) which would be raised by God would be 'spiritual' (*pneumatikon*). By this he meant that it would be like the body of Jesus in heaven, where Jesus is 'a life-giving spirit' (*pneuma*). In this spiritual, imperishable glory the body of 'flesh' (*sarx*) which had died in humiliation and weakness would be transformed, for 'flesh and blood can never possess the Kingdom of God and the perishable cannot possess immortality'. The flesh is not completely despised: it 'comes first' in every human life. But it is made of earth and its life is only *psychikon*. This word is derived from the use of *psyche* to mean 'life force' or 'vitality' and it can be translated as 'animal' (in the New English Bible) or even as 'physical' (in the Revised English Bible and the New Revised Standard Version). What is *pneumatikon* is greatly superior to what is *psychikon*.

There is a connection. In *Paradise Now and Not Yet* (1981),

Andrew Lincoln argued in detail and persuasively that although we do not know exactly what were the beliefs held by Christians in Corinth 'it seems highly likely that the Corinthians thought of the future in terms of continuing the reign they were already enjoying'. When Christ returned to earth in the near future 'they would simply continue to reign with him'. So 'they had made no provision in their thought for death and for what would happen to the body in this eventuality'. But Paul insisted that they must take the bodies which now gave them their personal identity with a seriousness which must change many of their attitudes. Life in the *psychikon* body is, he emphasized, a preparation for the higher life in the *pneumatikon* body. But there is also a great contrast between the two bodies. As James Dunn wrote in his fine study of *The Theology of Paul the Apostle* (1998), 'the point for us could scarcely be clearer' and it is the point that 'redemption for Paul was . . . a transformation into a different kind of bodily existence . . . not fleshly body, or body made of dust, or corruptible body, or mortal body'. Paul taught these Corinthians to hope for 'an embodiment appropriate to the world of the Spirit, beyond death'. But 'quite what Paul envisaged we can hardly begin to say'. What is certain is that, as Professor Dunn and many other scholars have pointed out, Paul did not confine his use of the word 'body' (*soma*) to references to a physical body: for example, he prominently called the Church, a spiritual fellowship, 'the body of Christ'.

It is also certain that Paul did not make any clear statement that the *pneumatikon* bodies of the Christian dead would be like the resurrected body of Jesus which had escaped from the tomb and had been seen in a physical shape by disciples, beginning with women. A possible explanation is that he did not wish to rely on evidence provided by women: no woman was included in the list of witnesses to the resurrection of Jesus which he transmitted to the Corinthians at the beginning of this chapter in his letter. But another explanation is also possible: he may not have believed that the resurrection of Jesus was physical. In this connection it is important to look closely at the list which he 'handed on' to his converts in Corinth about twenty years after the crucifixion.

The list has been constructed with great care, for belief in the resurrection of Jesus was of the utmost importance and witnesses to it became authorities in the churches. It was highly significant that 'Peter' should be named first (but as Cephas, not in the Greek version of his nickname Rock), followed by the rest of the 'Twelve' (although only eleven of the leading male disciples were left between the suicide of Judas and the election of Matthias). Then 'over five hundred of our brothers' are said to have seen the risen Lord, most being still alive to tell the story. It has been suggested by some scholars that the very first list of witnesses ended there, but when Paul transmitted the list to the Corinthians it included 'appearances' to James, the brother of the Lord who became the head of the church in Jerusalem, and to 'all the apostles', a group of leaders wider than the Twelve.

Then Paul adds:

> In the end he appeared even to me. It was like a birth after the normal time; I had persecuted the church of God and am therefore inferior to all the other apostles and not fit to be called an apostle. But by God's grace I am what I am and his grace had not been given to me in vain. On the contrary, I have worked harder than them all – although it was not I but the grace of God at work in me. (1 Corinthians 15:6–10)

It is obvious that Paul is being specially sensitive as he dictates or writes. He knows that his authority is rejected by critics. He has just asked the Corinthians: 'Am I not an apostle? Did I not see the Lord?' (9:1). But he never claims that the 'appearance' which was the turning point of his life, and the basis of all his later work, was physical. He told the Galatians only that 'God chose to reveal his son to me and through me' (1:16) and the Philippians only that 'Christ once took hold of me' (3:12). And the three slightly different accounts of this arresting revelation which are included in the Acts of the Apostles do not mention a body being seen. It is said that a light and a voice were sufficient to make Paul an apostle.

We have no other evidence about the encounter with Jesus which changed Paul's life and there must be uncertainty about the connection between this encounter and the accounts in the gospels of appearances by the risen Jesus which had a physical dimension. In the extensive discussion of the problem it has often been maintained that Paul must have believed that the resurrection of Jesus was physical, because (it has been claimed) no other kind of resurrection was conceivable by a Jew of that time. An acceptance of the reports about the discovery of the empty tomb may well be implied by Paul's acceptance of the tradition that Jesus 'was buried and that he was raised again on the third day according to the scriptures' – a tradition which seems to understand the resurrection as the fulfilment of the prediction of Hosea about the future of Israel quoted earlier in this book (6:2). An acceptance of the difference between Paul's own encounter and the earlier appearances of the risen body may well be implied by the admission that the encounter was 'like a birth after the normal time'. And some of the appearances related in the gospels may well be referred to in Paul's list. On the other hand, Paul does not say explicitly that there was any difference between the experiences of the other apostles and his own encounter. As we have seen, in that age Jews did not necessarily believe in a physical resurrection and there is no absolute proof that Paul believed that one had occurred when his living Lord had been 'raised'.

Perhaps the answer is that he had no wish to discuss the question. It may be relevant that a Christian prophet clothed his account of a vision of the glorious body of the risen Jesus not in an accurate photograph but in images taken from the Hebrew Bible. One Sunday John of Patmos had the experience of seeing a light 'like the sun in full strength' and of hearing a voice 'like the sound of a trumpet', which he understood as an encounter with 'Jesus Christ, the faithful witness, the first-born from the dead and the ruler of the kings of the earth'. He fell down 'as though dead' but by this appearance his 'Lord' proclaimed to him: 'I was dead and now I am alive for ever, and I hold the keys of Death and Death's Kingdom' (Revelation of John 1:9–18). It may be that both Paul and John of Patmos were content to know that the risen Jesus had the spiritual equivalent of physical embodiment – and to believe that this would be the future of others among the dead.

Writing again to Corinth about life after death (probably no more than a year after that earlier letter), Paul used different images. His eyes, he wrote, were fixed on the unseen, on the eternal. He now taught that if his tent-like earthly body were to be demolished, he would possess 'a building which God has provided – a house not made by human hands but eternal and heavenly'. He still valued his physical or *psychikon* body; he hoped to have the heavenly or *pneumatikon* body put over it (like an overcoat) in order that he should not find himself 'naked'. (This valuation of the physical is very Jewish, in a sharp contrast with the teaching in *Phaedo*, but also very Jewish is the horror of nakedness.) But whether or not that wish was to be granted, his deeper yearning was to 'leave our home in this body and go to live with the Lord' (2 Corinthians 4:18 – 5:10). In contrast with his earlier letter, he did not write of the need of his present body to be changed into his resurrection body. Nor did he say that until that resurrection the Christian dead would merely 'sleep', as he had told the Thessalonians: he spoke of life with the Lord in an 'eternal and heavenly glory'.

Writing to Philippi about five years after his first letter to Thessaloniki, he said that 'what I should like is to depart and be with Christ; that is better by far'. He would accept a continuing life on earth but only as the opportunity 'to know Christ, to experience the power of his resurrection, and to share his sufferings, in growing uniformity with his death, if only I may finally arrive at the resurrection from the dead' (3:10, 11). His earlier images of that resurrection were not repeated. Instead, this prisoner who now faced a nearer prospect of death hoped that his future body would be like the 'resplendent' body of Jesus, coming 'from heaven' to meet him. This, too, seems to be a hope for an 'eternal and heavenly' house but Paul had no ambition to describe the house's furniture or its change from the tent-like body of flesh made of earth. In his tantalizing reference to his highest mystical experience, in his second surviving letter to Corinth, he said only that he 'was caught up into the third heaven and heard words so secret that human lips may not repeat them'. 'Whether this was in the body or out of it I do not know – God knows' (12:1–5). He pressed on to repeat what he had learned about 'strength made perfect in weakness', Christ's strength in Paul's weak body.

He maintained this reticence about life after death in his longest letter, to the Christians in Rome. His main concern, now as always, was with the new moral and spiritual life before death. In chapter 8, this new life is known while we are in our mortal bodies because 'the Spirit' already lives in us, but this Spirit is 'the first fruits of the harvest to come', of 'the splendour, as yet unrevealed, which is in store for us'. All history and all nature are now 'as if in the pangs of childbirth' waiting for 'God's children to be revealed' in their 'liberty and splendour'. Paul did not say how the universe might be 'freed from the shackles of mortality' or how 'the redemption of our bodies' would be accomplished, but it is at least a possible interpretation of his vision to say that the universe will be immortal in the sense that its existence will have shaped the 'eternal and heavenly house' which will be the permanent home of each of the children of God. This would be compatible both with scientific knowledge about the nature of the physical universe and with the thought in the New Testament that, despite the hope for 'new heavens and a new earth, the home of justice', 'the present heavens and earth have been kept in store for burning' (2 Peter 3:7–13) and they must 'vanish' (Revelation 20:11).

It has often been claimed that a belief in the physical resurrection of Jesus is central in every part of the New Testament, and it is indeed the case that, for example, the First Letter of Peter begins with praise of 'the God and Father of our Lord Jesus Christ, who in his great mercy gave us new birth into a living hope by the resurrection of Jesus Christ from the dead' (1:3). But that document includes no account of any 'appearance' by Jesus to Peter, and in the New Testament there is also a tradition that Christ was 'exalted' to 'the right hand of the throne of God' without any specific mention of the resurrection. This tradition appears in the hymns quoted to the Philippians (2:6–11) and in the First Letter of Timothy (3:16). An argument from a brief document's, or a hymn's, silence on a particular subject is always dangerous, but it is remarkable that in the quite long Letter to Hebrews it is not said how Jesus was 'brought back from the dead' (13:20) although his glory now that he has 'passed through the heavens' (4:14) is the main theme, 'the resurrection of the dead' is part of the basic teaching given elsewhere (6:2), and it is recalled that in the history of the Jews 'women received back their dead by resurrection' (11:35).

It has often also been claimed that the narratives instruct us about our own future bodies, which will be 'like his'. But when studied, these stories can be seen to withhold this information. It seems to be possible, although certainly not necessary, to think that the meaning of 'the resurrection of the dead' is that 'the spirits of the righteous' are 'made perfect' (Hebrews 12:23).

The gospels in the New Testament did not narrate all of the 'appearances' of the risen Jesus in the tradition passed on by Paul to the Christians in Corinth. The event involving 'more than five hundred' was not among those stories, although it may be linked, or be identical, with the experience of the gift of the Holy Spirit related by Luke in Acts 2. The appearance to James was not mentioned. An appearance to Peter, which Paul puts first and which modern scholars inclined to scepticism tend to suggest was the vision which started the history of the Christian Church, was narrated only in the last chapter of the fourth gospel, which must be an epilogue added later. Mark's gospel, now generally agreed to have been the earliest, did not include any appearances at all – or at least did not unless it originally continued beyond 16:8, 'They said nothing to anybody, for they were afraid.' It seems very unlikely that Christians allowed the ending of this first gospel to be lost before Luke or Matthew could use it. There have been many guesses as to why Mark almost certainly ended with this anticlimax (and with the Greek *gar*, 'for') when he had included three predictions by Jesus of his resurrection. Did he not know of any reports of appearances? Did he not believe them? Or did he not use them, because he expected the appearances to be in the future? But it cannot be claimed that Mark believed the details of appearances which had occurred to be of decisive importance as he told 'the good news of Jesus Christ the Son of God' (1:1).

All four gospels report that women discovered that the tomb of Jesus was empty; only Luke says that the first appearance was to Peter and he does not describe it (24:34). They do not agree about the details. Mark says that Mary of Magdala, Mary the mother of James and Salome were given a message by an unexplained 'young man wearing a white robe' in the tomb, but Luke says that the two Marys and Joanna saw 'two men in dazzling garments', later understood by the other disciples as 'a vision of angels' (24:4, 23). Matthew says that the two Marys (only) saw one angel rolling away the stone at the entrance to the tomb amid a violent earthquake, but does not explain whether the stone had to be moved in order to let the women in or Jesus out. (The Gospel of Peter, which the Church rejected as spurious, told how three 'men' emerged from the tomb, two of them assisting the central figure who carried his cross in triumph.) The women then met Jesus, clasped his feet in adoration and heard him repeating what the angels told them. John says that the anonymous 'beloved disciple' and Peter saw 'linen wrappings' lying empty in the empty tomb (but Mark writes of a single 'linen sheet' at 15:46). Mary of Magdala had already made the discovery that the tomb was empty, without seeing any angel, but we are not told of any contact between her and the two men. She was soon told by Jesus himself to give to 'my brothers' the news that 'I am ascending'. This Mary is not mentioned in the Acts of the

Apostles, but in the conclusion added to Mark's gospel she, not Peter, was the first to see the risen Lord (16:9).

The gospels are equally disorganized in their reports about where and how the 'appearances' of the risen body took place. According to Mark and Matthew the women are told that 'he is going on before you into Galilee' and in Matthew's gospel 'the eleven disciples' do meet Jesus on a mountain in Galilee. In Luke's gospel and in the Acts of the Apostles, however, these apostles do not leave the neighbourhood of Jerusalem and in the fourth gospel two appearances occur in Jerusalem before a third in Galilee.

These gospels do not give a consistent account, let alone an explanation, of the physicality of the risen Jesus. In Luke's gospel Jesus seems so normal, and yet so different, that the disciples talk to him for some time about himself without realizing who he is; later he eats a piece of fish as they watch but is 'parted from them in the act of blessing'. In Matthew's gospel some of the disciples are 'doubtful' even when they see him, and in John's gospel Jesus can invite Thomas to feel his body and can cook breakfast, but can also come through locked doors. It seems clear that this body, if it was real, was very strange. It also seems clear that the stories are not always accurate history; for example, in Matthew's gospel many saints rise from their graves and are seen in Jerusalem, soldiers on guard at the tomb are bribed by the priests to say that they had been asleep (although sleeping on duty was punishable by death) and Jesus commands baptism 'in the name of the Father and the Son and the Holy Spirit', a formula unknown to Paul and to the Acts of the Apostles.

These disagreements have formed a part of the modern discussion about whether the tomb really was empty. On the one hand, it has been maintained that the disagreements are not significant in comparison with the basic agreement of all the gospels, supported by what is (on this view) the most likely meaning of Paul's 'he was raised' and accepted by the whole of the Christian Church until the rise of modern criticism. There are also arguments which are weaker because they come from silence, not from facts: we do not know of any proof by non-Christians discrediting the story, or of any veneration of the Christians of the full tomb. On the other hand, it can be argued that in a non-scientific world reports about 'appearances' which were visionary rather than physical could grow into stories of a physical resurrection. On this view, by the time that these stories had developed, the body of Jesus had decomposed in a common grave or (what seems less likely) had been removed from the tomb by a person or persons unknown.

The gospels which record the stories were written within 30 to 60 years of the crucifixion and their different details reflect either the traditions of different communities or else the editorial tendencies of the writers. What is clear is that no investigation which would satisfy a modern detective had been done, although already when he wrote, Matthew felt that he had to mention and answer a story that the disciples had stolen and hidden the corpse (27:62–66). In the second century, the Roman writer Celsus was among the mockers. The appearances, he wrote, were the illusions of 'some hysterical women' or perhaps a man 'had a mistaken notion as has happened to thousands, or (as is more likely) wanted to impress others by telling this fantastic tale'. In the next century Tertullian mentioned with scorn a suggestion that the tomb in the garden had been emptied by the gardener in irritation that his vegetables were being ruined by visitors. The serious point being made by the Church's enemies was, of course, that the story of the empty tomb could easily be dismissed by people who had no cause provided by their own religious experience or heritage to believe it.

Therefore, modern people seriously interested in the historical evidence for an event which has usually been presented as an event in history are likely to conclude that Peter, Paul and some others did have visions of Jesus as alive and as 'Lord' after his cruel death. It is possible for a verdict based on the historical evidence to be that these visions were among the 'visual and auditory hallucinations' which can be said by psychologists to be the realities behind ghost stories or incidents investigated by parapsychology. It is, however, also possible to say that the historical evidence includes proof that these visions were not mere hallucinations, for they had the effect of transforming people – of inspiring Paul's life and surviving letters, for example. And almost all Christians have wished in the past, as many still do wish, to go beyond such verdicts because a fuller acceptance of the stories in the gospels, including the reports about the empty tomb, results from an acceptance of the faith that Jesus, while fully human, was also the embodiment of God in a human life; therefore, by a further mighty act of God, the victory of that life over death could be utterly unique in its character. This uniqueness could take the form of a new kind of embodiment, physical enough to make the impact on the disciples to which the New Testament bears witness. This new embodiment of Jesus could be God's own proclamation of the supremely important fact that his 'kingdom', the central theme of the message of Jesus before his death, could never be defeated and was indeed being established within human experience. Thus the resurrection was a vital part of the total triumph of God and nothing less than that has been, and is, celebrated by the Church which would never have existed had Jesus not been raised from the dead bodily at the beginning of the new creation.

All these things are still being said in our own time by intelligent people of high moral and spiritual quality. There must be a choice between these positions, however, and like other forms of belief or disbelief in life after death it depends on what is the thinker's general view of the world – the view which is brought into focus by a reaction to a miracle-story. Are all stories about miracles mere mistakes, or do they refer to momentous changes which can be explained within the categories of the sciences, or are they quite possibly 'true' in the sense that they astonishingly but actually occurred? In modern societies, many who sincerely wish to be counted as Christians have held the first or the second of these positions, while almost all the churches have continued to affirm the third as orthodoxy, as Easter, the queen of festivals, celebrates the king of miracles.

What seems unreasonable is to make a claim which is contradicted by the evidence. It should not be claimed that all the references to this resurrection deserve to be dismissed with contempt, for they are references to the events which began the astounding history of Christianity. Nor should it be claimed that the evidence enables us to say precisely 'what really happened' and then draw conclusions, for example the conclusion that because his corpse was reanimated mine will be. I have found myself, over many years, unable to settle my mind in any one of the three positions just outlined, but I have found wisdom in teaching such as that of an Anglican archbishop, Michael Ramsey, in his *The Resurrection of Christ* (1945): 'If it was "vision", it was vision created not from within themselves but by Jesus in his own objective impact on them and . . . if it was "bodily", it was with a big difference as belonging to a new order of existence.'

What, then, is the relevance for our concern in this book?

Adolf von Harnack, a great and critical historian of the Church, said at the beginning of the twentieth century: 'Whatever may have happened at the grave and in the matter of the appearances, one thing is certain: this grave was the birth-place of the indestructible belief that death is vanquished, that there is life eternal.' Emil Brunner, a Protestant theologian who valued orthodoxy more highly as a result of Europe's experiences in the first half of that century, saw the resurrection of Jesus as a hole in history of which only the edges are clearly facts of history, but he added that through this hole the light of 'the eternal hope' shines. Hans Küng, a Catholic theologian with a passion for truth, wrote in *Eternal Life?* (1984): 'Neither Jesus's resurrection nor ours is dependent on an empty tomb. The reanimation of a corpse is not a precondition for rising to eternal life . . . Christian life therefore appeals not to the empty tomb but to the encounter with the living Christ himself'.

Peter Carnley, an Anglican archbishop who made a detailed study of *The Structure of Resurrection Belief* (1987), concluded that

> the first appearances took the form of 'heavenly visions' or Christophanies of the raised and glorified Christ and that when, in the ensuing weeks and years, attempts were made to express the 'heavenly vision' or 'appearance' in verbal form, a variety of different images was used . . . The unity of the story is the truth of the disposition or character of Christ which is revealed in and through the myriad diverse episodes of the scriptural story to those who have an eye to see and an ear to hear . . . The various and diverse aspects are to the communication of the truth concerning Jesus himself, as the variety of the colours of the spectrum are to the white light.

Any touches of the imagination in these Easter stories come from hearts and minds upon which this white light has shone, for to a Christian 'the truth concerning Jesus himself' carries with it the truth about resurrection in reality. When Jesus explains that the Messiah was 'bound to suffer before entering upon his glory' in Luke's gospel, the Christian is shown that the One who in the Acts of the Apostles is called 'the Lord of glory' humbly followed the tough pattern of all human life. When Jesus is known to the disciples as 'he took bread and said the blessing', the Christian knows that the Eucharist is the drama where an extremely painful death is celebrated because it was overcome. When Jesus tells the disciples that he has 'full authority in heaven and earth' in Matthew's gospel, he tells all the generations that the life embodied in him, the life of God, is stronger than anything during or after life in the flesh which suffers and dies. When Jesus speaks to the weeping woman in the garden, according to the fourth gospel, he calls her by her name: 'Mary!' His greeting implies an assurance that her personal identity is, and will be, maintained by God: although it has been shaped by a life in a body which in the language of the time is said to have been possessed by 'seven devils' (Luke 8:2). So the gospel's 23 references to 'eternal life' are now addressed to her personally. When Jesus invites doubting Thomas to inspect the wounds inflicted by the crucifixion, this assurance about the victory of God and about eternal life comes from inside knowledge of what human suffering and dying mean: the Jesus who is rightly called 'Lord and God' is entitled to speak as he does about life and death because he has gone through them. When Jesus assures Peter of forgiveness and of work to do, he sets free the Christian Church to be a witness to the unlimited grace of God despite its own great faults. And when Jesus invites Peter to 'follow me', he commands not only a young man with the world before him but also the person who 'when you are old' will meet those who 'will bind you fast and carry you where you have no wish to go', to death.

In none of these stories is it claimed that Jesus gave detailed information about life after death: nowhere does he promise his disciples that they will have bodies like the body now in front of them. But it is plain that the character-sketch provided by the New Testament is very different from the portrait of Socrates in Plato's *Phaedo* and from the aloofness to life and death advocated by Krishna in the *Bhagavad Gita*. Jesus of Nazareth was a man who valued everyday physical life so highly that his main method when teaching about God was to tell stories based on what was going on around him. He was deserted by his friends and was afraid of the cruel death which awaited him. The Letter to Hebrews says that 'in taking death he represented us all' in order that he might 'liberate those who, through fear of death, had been slaves all their lives' (2:9, 15). 'He offered up prayers and petitions, with loud cries and tears, to God who was able to deliver him from the grave' (5:7). He was delivered, but only after he had passed through that 'school of suffering' (5:8). He was not delivered by his own intellectual ability or moral goodness. He did not rise above death in a human triumph. He was raised by the power of God. Now he can be met on any road in the world and whenever he is met God the Father is also met, for he is the living Word of the Father. By living, dying and appearing after death Jesus expressed the supreme characteristic of the Father, patiently faithful love – and to those who have really met him, he still does, amid all this life's perplexities and sorrows. Moreover, he is in eternity the human person who to other humans is the 'human face' of the Eternal.

The stories told about the 'appearances' of Jesus after his terrible death suggest neither that his mission was to satisfy curiosity about heaven or hell, nor that he had found eternity to be Nirvana where the brief candle of a human life is given the peace of extinction, nor that he was being absorbed back into Nature or the Infinite. His message was summed up as 'I am ascending to my Father and your Father, my God and your God' (John 20:17).

9

Hell as Love

WHAT ABOUT THOSE who do not 'ascend to heaven'? The question needs to be faced because 'the traditional idea of hell has been banished to the far-off corners of the Christian mind'. So a Victorian prime minister, Gladstone, said, and the claim seems to be more accurate now than it was when he made it. Here is a change of very great importance, for during most of its history the Christian mind has been full of the pornographic horror of the torture chamber in which most men and women (and children?) will suffer and scream for all eternity. No other religion has put such emphasis on hell's unending agonies. In the Hindu tradition may be found highly alarming pictures of many hells; the Buddhist tradition has also extended the suffering of life before death to suffering after it; and the exercise of power on earth in China's long history as an empire was more than matched by beliefs about the imperial power of demons afflicting the dead. But, outside traditional Christianity, hell has seldom been believed to involve permanent pain of excruciating intensity: usually it was hoped that there would come a moment of release, even if it was only release into another life of suffering on earth. The prominence of the idea of an everlasting hell in the history of Christianity is equalled only in the history of Islam, where this emphasis may well be among the beliefs learned from Christians. So an immense change has occurred. Today, probably most Christians believe that any true and enduring content in the idea of hell consists of the beliefs that some may decide to reject God's love finally and that, out of love, out of respect for his children's freedom, God may accept that rejection with (so to speak) a broken heart of love. If anyone were to make that ultimate rejection, it would carry with it the rejection of God-given life. It would mean the 'second death' of the dead. It would be, for that one, the end.

The downfall of the traditional idea was due mainly to moral indignation about its cruelty. This objection was still applicable even when, in response to this indignation, hell was redefined as solitary confinement, avoiding the more material and social suffering which had excited the imaginations of many generations, for it was still not easy to describe as 'good' the divine Judge who inflicted an endless punishment of this sort on a creature made to be sociable. Such a creature would be bound to go endlessly mad. 'I will call no Being good', said John Stuart Mill in a protest which had many echoes, 'who is not what I mean when I apply that epithet to my fellow creatures, and if such a Being can sentence me to Hell for not so calling him, than to Hell I will go.' Such insolence to the Judge of all the world shocked many but it was more widely felt to be shocking that the Judge had been portrayed as the collaborator in a sadism which had no limits.

Hell has been believed to be the final destiny of the vast majority of humankind. It has been held by teachers of orthodoxy that the few who will be spared will be thoroughly orthodox Christians (of a particular kind of orthodoxy), or saints with a track record of exceptionally good deeds, or simply God's predestined favourites. As we have noted, in the orthodox system a single 'mortal' sin could earn an eternity in hell. In the days of red-blooded belief, hell could be described as an overcrowded, foul-smelling, infernally noisy place where sinners could suffer for an infinite period of time, with bodies resurrected in order to add to the agonies inflicted by devils, fire, wind, sewage, worms, snakes, toads, dragons, chains and thick darkness (for this fire would give no light). Hell could be located in the middle of the heat of the sun but the usual preference was for the centre of the earth, with hints of its fires erupting from volcanoes. Those condemned would regret their damnable stupidity but repentance, or some lesser form of moral improvement, would be impossible after death.

It cannot be known exactly how far this accumulation of horrors was a deterrent against sin (already in the Middle Ages the images of hell could be enjoyed as material for comedy). It could nevertheless be claimed that the fear of this truly terrible punishment 'peopled heaven' and we know that Hamlet was not the only miserable person to feel 'the dread of something after death' and therefore not commit the sin of suicide. Nightmares about hell seem to have been fairly common and the fear could be great in the minds of the most vulnerable – the immature, the unbalanced, the hypersensitive and the dying. People who did not expect this to be their own destination could accept it as the just punishment of others and when proposals arose for the removal of hell's unending tortures from the list of the compulsory doctrines of Christianity, many of the good and the great feared that a public discussion, let alone a change in the Church's teaching, would remove the public's incentive to control lust, greed and other evil passions. Hell, it was feared, would be let loose on earth. There might also be a revolution in society. It is also certain the Catholic and Protestant missionaries faced distances, dangers and deaths in order to rescue the heathen from hell. They could not have provided clearer evidence that to them the danger was real.

In the eighteenth century, Jonathan Edwards kept in touch with scientific and philosophical thought and he is often reckoned to have been the most eminent American theologian. But he warned sinners about hell: 'If you cry to God to pity you, he will only tread you under foot. He will crush you under his feet without mercy; he will crush out your blood and make it fly and it shall be sprinkled on his garments so as to stain all his garments.' In 1728 he preached that 'the least sin deserves eternal destruction' but that it would not be a quick end: in hell 'the creature has as much misery as the nature can receive' in 'the extreme degree of torment'. For example, the damned will be 'always burning and roasting in a fire and yet never able to die, yea, to have the senses preserved in every part of the body in their usual quickness'. Being a scholar he acknowledged that he had to use images but he maintained that he drew them from Holy Scripture and that 'when metaphors are used in Scripture about spiritual things, the things of another world, they fall short of the literal truth'. Thus he claimed to be understating the actual horrors.

James Joyce drew on a pamphlet by a Catholic priest when, remembering his own schooldays in Ireland, he described the instruction given to the young Stephen Dedalus in his *Portrait of the Artist as a Young Man* (1916). The preacher would no doubt agree with the description of hell in the Roman Catechism of 1564 as 'that most loathsome and dark prison in which the souls of the damned together with the unclean spirits are tortured in everlasting and inextinguishable fire'. He would not disagree with the teaching of that official catechism that all who are not baptized, 'whether their parents are Christians or infidels, are born to eternal misery and everlasting damnation', but he is preaching to Catholic schoolboys in danger of sinning mortally. So, with no danger of understatement, he explains that 'the sulphurous brimstone which burns in hell is a substance which is specially designed to burn for ever and ever with unspeakable fury', with the result that 'the blood seethes and boils in the veins, the brains are boiling in the skull, the heart in the breast glowing and bursting, the bowels a red hot mass of burning pulp, the tender eyes flaming . . . ' But fire will not be the only torture, for 'the filth of the world shall run there as to a vast and reeking sewer' while 'the damned howl and scream against each other'.

An audience younger than Stephen Dedalus was addressed by an Irish priest, John Joseph Furniss, in *The Sight of Hell* (1864). Children were urged to learn from the sight of 'the little child in the red-hot oven', screaming and beating its head against the roof. 'God was very good to this little child' because, had he not 'called it out of the world in early childhood', it might have 'got worse and worse' and 'would have been punished more severely'.

The great theologians who have been less enthusiastic as lecturers in conducted tours of hell, but who have emphatically believed in its endless punishments, include the saints Augustine and Thomas Aquinas and the reformers Luther and Calvin. This list does not include the great name of Origen, who was condemned by the Church (formally in a council in 543) mainly because he had taught that although many souls would undergo a painful education after their deaths, possibly involving reincarnation, it was reasonable to hope that in the end all would be saved by the mercy of God. It is, however, difficult to know precisely what were Origen's conclusions, for much of what he wrote was destroyed or preserved only after censorship. In any case, orthodoxy stood firm and was repeated in 1530 in the Augsburg Confession, which was intended to reassure Catholics that Protestants were not heretics: 'God will condemn impious people and devils to torture without end' (Article 17).

Augustine and Aquinas were also understood as teaching that God predestined people to hell whatever they thought or did, although Augustine was not so clear about this as he was about predestination to heaven, and Aquinas added that he allowed them to choose what sins to commit so that this punishment would obviously be deserved. This speculation was never endorsed by any council of the Church, in East or West, and many Lutherans who took advantage of some obscurity in Luther's own teaching also refused to accept it. However, orthodox Calvinists have felt bound by the insistence of their master that 'double predestination' is the case. Calvin seems to have felt appalled to find himself teaching this *horribile* (fearsome) doctrine, but he taught it.

It was, he claimed, 'highly absurd' to say that God 'elected' some to heaven while 'others acquire by chance, or obtain by their own efforts, what God's choice alone confers on a few'. The truth seemed to him to be that 'God wills to exclude' this majority of humankind from 'the inheritance which he predestines for his own children'. And the damned who are 'bound over before their begetting to everlasting calamity' cannot complain since 'all of us are vitiated by sin and we can only be odious to God . . . by the fairest reckoning of justice'. Calvin based himself largely on a brief passage in the letter to Rome where Paul, deeply depressed by the moral disorder of the pagan world and by the refusal of most Jews to accept Jesus as the Messiah, allowed himself to speculate around the image of God as a potter who goes on moulding clay which in the end he knows he cannot use. He asked: 'What if God, desiring to show his retribution at work and to make known his power, tolerated very patiently objects which are made for retribution and destruction?' (9:22). But Calvin swept aside the all-embracing optimism at the end of this section of Paul's letter: 'When he made all to be prisoners of sin, God's purpose was to be merciful to all . . . How unsearchable are his judgements, how untraceable his ways!' (11:32, 33). That optimism was also expressed in Paul's belief that the result of God's 'act of grace' in Christ is 'acquittal and life for all' (Romans 5:18), so that 'in Christ all will be made alive' (1 Corinthians 15:22), and it is echoed in dimensions no smaller than the universe in the later letters to the Ephesians (1:10) and the Colossians (1:20). It is a fair summary of Pauline teaching, taken as a whole, to say that it is the will of 'God our Saviour' that 'everyone should be saved' (1 Timothy 2:4).

Later, it was often taught that God would rejoice to see the execution of his justice in hell. So would the angels and the saints: as Thomas Aquinas said, the saints will be granted 'a perfect view of the punishment of the damned in order that they may enjoy their beatitude more thoroughly and give more abundant thanks for it'. Tertullian, who on earth was no saint, hoped to be in their company.

> How shall I admire, how laugh, how rejoice, how exult when I behold . . . so many magistrates liquefying in fiercer flames than they ever kindled against the Christians, so many wise philosophers blushing in red-hot fires with their deluded pupils . . . so many dancers tripping more nimbly from anguish than they ever managed when there was applause.

Meanwhile he was happy to think that hell would be 'more frightening than any human murder'. More soberly, Pope Gregory the Great taught in the sixth century that 'no mercy affects the minds of the elect' because 'they see the justice of the punishment of the damned and cannot regret it'. But, after 1,500 years or more of Christian history, voices began to be heard in protest.

At first the protests were too dangerously associated with other heresies to be heeded, or for safety's sake they were kept from the public. There was also confusion among hell's critics: would the wicked eventually be annihilated or saved? But in Protestant England protests gradually surfaced. In 1690 a future Archbishop of Canterbury, John Tillotson, included in a sermon the thought that God was not morally bound to carry out threats of everlasting tortures: actually to preside over hell was something which 'no good man would do'. Gradually, many English Christians ceased to believe what had been taken for granted: that punishments are chiefly intended to bring retribution to the offender, that they are rightly graded according to the status of the person offended, that an offended God is entitled to infinite retribution, that Adam did offend God and that every human being ever born has inherited Adam's guilt. Punishments, it was now thought, should show that certain behaviour is condemned by God or by society, but they should not be merely vindictive; they should be adjusted to the gravity of the crime itself and not to the status of the person offended; and where possible they should result in the reformation of the offender. The story of Adam and Eve came to be regarded as a myth and an individual's sin to be treated as his or her own fault. But it was increasingly felt that many people were not entirely to blame for their faults, that to some extent they could not help themselves in their circumstances. As the eighteenth century became the nineteenth, Thomas Belsham attacked William Wilberforce for believing in 'a Being who first forms his creatures with a nature radically depraved and then condemns the majority of them to eternal misery for being what he himself made them'. And in the infant USA, a small part of the declaration of political independence was an independence in religion which included some congregations explicitly calling themselves Universalist because in the end salvation must be universal.

The English debate exploded after 1850. F. D. Maurice, Victorian England's most creative theologian, maintained that while to be 'alienated from goodness and truth' would mean being 'in the deepest pit of hell', the Greek word *aionios*, translated in the authorized English version of the New Testament as 'everlasting', did not necessarily mean 'endless'. Conservatives replied that often this was the obvious meaning of a passage in the Greek, and that no person teaching that the punishments of hell might not be endless was fit to teach future clergymen. So Maurice was deprived of his professorship. It was a muddled controversy since *aionios* is itself a translation of the adjective of the Hebrew noun *olam* used in the phrase 'the age to come'; *olam* could also refer to the world or the universe and its essential content was largeness. In his letter to Philemon, Paul could send a runaway slave back to his master for an *aionios* period which would be long but limited by death, although the *aion* in 'the age to come' was the final age. Thus the appeal to language about hell met with ambiguity. There is a similar ambiguity in much of our use of the phrase 'for ever'.

Before long another Anglican clergyman, H. B. Wilson, made public his hope that at the Last Judgement 'receptacles' would be found where 'infants as to spiritual development' might make enough progress so that eventually all might 'find refuge in the bosom of the Universal Parent, to repose or to be quickened into higher life'. Eleven thousand clergymen of the Church of England indignantly endorsed 'the words of our Blessed Lord, that the "punishment" of the "cursed", equally with the "life" of the "righteous", is everlasting', but the Judicial Committee of the Privy Council refused to condemn as a crime 'the expression of a hope by a clergyman that even the ultimate pardon of the wicked . . . may be consistent with the will of Almighty God'.

In 1877 another Anglican clergyman, F. W. Farrar, preached in Westminster Abbey about Eternal Hope, maintaining that a person's destiny was not 'finally and irrevocably sealed at death'. If someone were to resist improvement permanently, and were to be condemned to hell, that punishment might not be as pictured and might not be endless. Although the prospect of an end to the suffering of the wicked again aroused many protests, the criticism of crude hell-fire preaching gained more sympathy and by the end of the century preachers and writers were spreading the beliefs that progress was possible after death and that, since immortality was God's gift, the gift could rightly be withdrawn from anyone who to the end refused to accept God's love. Education after death would be strenuous, but there would be no endless torture. These critics of hell were influenced by the Victorian belief in progress through education (and perhaps also by the Darwinian belief in the survival of the fittest), but over a long period the situation developed in which a theologian in the mainstream of religious thought, Brian Hebblethwaite, could write in *The Christian Hope* (1984):

> It does, from any point of view, seem very hard indeed to see how Christian theology can go on affirming the objective reality of a state or sphere of everlasting loss and self-inflicted alienation for some of God's creatures within the final, consummated state of the whole creative process. Such permanent evil makes no religious or moral sense.

And historians have agreed that the experience of the First World War discredited belief in hell more effectively than any preacher's or theologian's new teaching. The conditions under which soldiers lived and died in France and Flanders were similar to the conditions in hell as traditionally preached and pictured, and it became incredible that such conditions reflected the will of God the Father. Moreover, it could not be honestly believed that the soldiers who were killed in these battles, which seemed to have no end and little point, were mostly saints; yet it became unthinkable that the divinely perfect Judge should transfer them from hell on earth to hell in eternity. Instead, war memorials permanently honoured the dead as martyrs, whose listed names were sacred. Thus, in the minds of many, hell died in that war.

In Roman Catholic circles other developments banished, or at least minimized, the traditional idea of tortures after death. As we saw when looking at the *Catechism of the Catholic Church*, by the 1990s the emphasis in teaching about hell had moved to 'separation from God', and purgatory, the traditional 'third place' between heaven and hell, had become more clearly a condition of purification, not timed punishment.

The idea of purgatory arose from the natural belief that most people die neither as saints nor as entirely wicked sinners. For example Perpetua, a young Christian woman who was martyred in 203, knew that her brother, who had died of cancer at the age of seven, had not been a Christian so would not be in heaven. But during her imprisonment a dream of his continuing pain persuaded her to pray for his release and a second dream persuaded her to believe that her prayer had been granted. A solution to the problem of what awaited such souls was found by developing the idea that they might not go immediately either to heaven or to hell. It was natural to think of death as 'sleep'; the gospels show that a girl who was asleep could be thought to be dead (Mark 5:39) and that a man who was dead could be said to be asleep (John 11:11–15). Tertullian developed this into the concept of the *refrigerium interim*, a refreshing sleep before being admitted to heaven by the Last Judgement. But then it was seen that if the sleepers were awakened, and made capable of receiving punishments or rewards, this 'interim state' would solve the problem. Some 200 years after Perpetua, the great Augustine prayed for his dead mother Monica and named this 'interim state': in it there could be punishments not permanent but *purgatoria*.

In earlier years it had been felt that no serious sin committed by a Christian, once forgiven and baptized, would ever be forgiven: that was taught in the Letter to Hebrews (6:4) and the First Letter of John (5:16). It therefore seems likely that the commission to forgive sins in the Easter gospel of John (20:23) refers to forgiveness through baptism. But gradually the Church recognized that many baptized Christians remained sinners; that when attached by family ties or friendship they wished to pray for the dead who might still be guilty; and that even serious sins could be forgiven if the sinner repented. Western Catholics therefore developed a system by which sins could be confessed and absolved. For many years the confession had to be made in public, and forgiveness was granted only if a rigorous period of 'penance' was completed. Then private confession to a priest became normal, and in 1215 it was made compulsory once a year. Sinners who had been forgiven by a priest could accept that the punishments which their sins still deserved would take years to complete and that some of these years could lie beyond death. The dead could do nothing to help themselves but the prayers of the Church could assist in shortening the time needed; it could be explained that the sufferings of Christ had been more 'copious' than anything needed to reconcile the Father so that the surplus, a 'treasury of merits', had been accumulated and entrusted to the Church for use. Bishops and theologians still insisted that some sins were so serious that if not fully repented they deserved hell, but public opinion preferred to concentrate on the possibility of forgiveness after punishment: that, after all, was how children were treated. The birth of 'purgatory' was more or less complete in the twelfth century and was registered by a church council at Lyons in 1274.

The Greek and Russian Orthodox still objected to legislating about matters which were best left to God, as they had been in the older teachings, and the Protestant protests in the sixteenth century expressed an unease already felt by many Catholics: there was no biblical basis for the new system and it could be trivialized into a bargain about 'years in purgatory' with payments to the clergy for their services in reducing the sentence.

In the nineteenth century thoughtful Catholics such as Cardinal Newman persisted in believing that there needed to be a third 'state' for the dead in addition to heaven and hell. (To meet this need some Protestants had been found to use the idea of 'degrees' of glory or pain in the two states, which did have solid scriptural foundations.) But now the emphasis was not on punishment in purgatory with pains which, as had been taught by the leading authorities, were worse than any pain ever experienced on earth. Nor was the stress on the time needed for this treatment. Newman's *Dream of Gerontius* (1865) was thus very different from Dante's medieval *Purgatorio*. On the mountain of purgatory as in the depths of hell, Dante's imagination worked overtime and with superb skill, naming the sinners and creating forms of punishment which corresponded neatly with their sins. It may even be thought that despite his disclaimers Dante enjoyed himself as he acted in the place of God. But Newman was far more restrained as he indicated what would be for Gerontius a short period of sleep in a lake, cleansing the soul in preparation for heaven. The angel who gently lowers the soul into this bath of 'happy' pain sings

> Swiftly shall pass thy night of trial here,
> And I will come and wake thee on the morrow.

A difficulty which thoughtful Catholics now saw clearly was that the 'holy souls' in purgatory had already been forgiven by the divinely authorized representatives of the Church on earth: to think that they still deserved agonizing punishments might be like imagining that the prodigal son should have been sent to a long spell in prison after the welcome by his father. The solution to this difficulty might well be to think of purgatory as the Father himself, in his sterner side. 'Purgatory', says Hans Küng, 'is God himself in the wrath of his grace.'

So what did the New Testament actually teach?

A close study of it will show that it is far less bloodthirsty than many preachers and artists have been. The second chapter of the document called the Second Letter of Peter is a robust denunciation of the wicked: it does not hesitate to say that perdition is the destiny of misleading teachers and that a fearsome punishment awaits 'those who follow their own abominable lusts'. But we do not read of endless tortures, simply of exclusion from the light of God: 'the place reserved for them is blackest darkness'.

Paul wrote very little about the fate of the wicked, never mentioning the Greek version of the Hebrew word for hell, *Gehenna*. *The Apocalypse of Paul*, a detailed description of hell, dates from the 380s (and develops *The Apocalypse of Peter*, a vision of hell early in the second century), but even in that spurious 'revelation' Paul sighs over the tortures of the damned. He is rebuked by an angel: 'Are you more merciful than God?' Among his authentic writings, his first letter to Thessaloniki taught without explanation that already 'retribution has overtaken' those who persecuted Christians, so that the Day of the Lord would bring about their destruction (2:16, 5:3). His second letter warned that those who 'trouble' the Christians because they do not know God and do not obey the Gospel will 'suffer the punishment of eternal destruction, separated from the presence of the Lord and from the glory of his might' (1:6–12). His first letter to Corinth warned that a man's work might be burned and he himself might need to be 'saved by fire' (3:15) and his second letter warned that 'all of us must appear before the judgement seat of Christ, so that each may receive recompense for what he has done in the body, whether good or evil' (5:10). In neither letter was he more specific. His letter to Rome warned of the 'anguish' awaiting those who are utterly selfish, who refuse to accept what they see as a truth and who treat as evil their guide (2:8, 9), but the wicked would 'perish' (2:1) and this 'wrath and fury' of God would bring 'destruction', not endless tortures (9:22). In his tremendous denunciation of homosexual behaviour in the introduction to this letter, the most frightening thing he wrote was that 'God has given them up to the vileness of their own desires' and has 'given them up to the deformity of their own reason', leading to the death which they deserve (1:24–32). Here he echoed the many passages in the Hebrew Bible where the wrath of God against sin is expressed by saying that Yahweh 'hides his face', 'turns away' or 'surrenders' his people. There are many other passages where the wrath of God is said to be more active, sending an army or a plague to punish Israel, but these passages are questioned within the Hebrew Bible (supremely in the Book of Job), where the protest is made that no automatic connection exists between wickedness and suffering, and Paul refuses to go into details about how the wrath of God is exerted.

The gospels contain more material than Paul's letters do about the possibility of destruction after death, but not so much as is often claimed. Again we find solemn warnings, here reinforced by traditional imagery which Paul, it seems, avoided. However, the central teaching is not that death is near. It is that the Kingdom of God is 'near' on earth, as was the emphasis in Paul's first letter to the Thessalonians; the dawn of this kingdom on earth is what constitutes the crisis dividing light from darkness. An incident which is startling when seen in the context of current beliefs occurs both in Luke's gospel (9:59–61) and in Matthew's. A would-be disciple asks Jesus that he may be allowed to stay at home until his father has been buried; it is not said whether or not the father is still alive, but clearly he is near burial. For a son to secure a fitting burial for a father was regarded as a sacred duty, which was probably often influenced by the belief, widespread in the ancient world, that this action would determine the father's afterlife. With a dramatic proclamation of the urgency of his message to the living, Jesus replies: 'Let the dead bury their own dead but you go and proclaim the Kingdom of God.'

There is a considerable, although not complete, difference between this message about heaven coming to the earth and the message which created Islam.

Both Jesus and Muhammad were intensely concerned to reach and convert their hearers and to teach a new way of life before death, and as Jesus proclaimed his message in terms of the government of God, so Muhammad formed by word and action a community where 'submission' (the meaning of *Islam*) would be the response to the revelation of the will of God which he 'recited' (the meaning of *Quran*). But while Jesus addressed Jews who already believed in One God and were already regulated by the Law of Moses, the mission of the Prophet of Islam was to pagans who worshipped many divinities – roundly called 'idols' in the Quran. Life, they believed, was ruled by Fate and ended by death, although the equality of half-life might follow. Their morals were so undisciplined that the Quran had to contain a large number of new, strict and detailed commandments, later to be supplemented by the *haddith*, a large collection of the Prophet's sayings and practices. The success of Muhammad was immense. The revelations which he 'recited' formed on any showing one of the greatest books in the world, sustaining a level of eloquence and imagery so high that even non-Muslims ought to be able to see why the Quran is revered as the Word of God and why the Prophet's international impact has been so extensive.

Muhammad was also a military commander whose victory over the unbelieving Quraysh at Badr was decisive, and the stunning rapidity of the spread of Islam over the Middle East and North Africa obviously owed much to the use of force. But the spread of Islam elsewhere has often depended on the influence of the convictions of its lay adherents and in particular on the impressiveness of the passionate promises and warnings in the Quran about the Hour, the Day of Reckoning and Resurrection (as in the terrifying *sura* 81). Then, one by one, the dead will be commanded 'Read your record!' and will be sharply and permanently divided by the One God into those sent to Paradise and those sent to hell. Both destinations are pictured (for example in *sura* 55) in images which Arabs of the desert (but not only they) would readily understand. Muslim mystics and philosophers have expounded these images without treating them as physical, but probably for most people they have been powerful because physical. In Paradise there will be gardens and fountains, trees and fruit, garments of silk and rich brocade, soft couches and delicious food, silver and gold, ginger-flavoured water and the purest wine, with the (much discussed) 'dark-eyed *houris*, chaste as hidden pearls'. All these are symbols of 'peace' and 'light' and 'acceptance'. In hell the damned who 'cannot die' will receive punishments which are also symbolic –

chained amid the fire's extreme heat and power, suffering also through scorching winds and pitch-black smoke, fed on filth and made to drink boiling water 'as the thirsty camel drinks'. 'As often as their skins are consumed by the fire, We will replace them with new skins, that they may feel the torment' (4:59).

In the Quran the judgement of Allah (God) is the main theme. But in some passages it is qualified by two factors: the good and the evil alike have been predestined to their fates before their conceptions, yet the evil can be forgiven if before death they repent. Allah is 'the Merciful, the Compassionate', as is repeated at the beginning of each *sura* or chapter (although 'Clement' may be a better translation since 'Compassionate' suggests the sympathy of fellow-suffering). But after death there is justice, not mercy, and the judgement by the Lord of the Day of Doom concentrates on good or evil actions. 'Whosoever has done an ant's weight of good shall see it and whosoever has done an ant's weight of evil shall see it' (99:7, 8). 'Allah created death and life that he might test which of you is best in works' (67:2). In the *haddith*, however, the mercy of Allah can be exercised after death; after intercession by the Prophet there can be a pardon in the judgement or release from hell.

Muslim customs apply these teachings to the dying and the dead. The simple creed of Islam, 'there is no deity but Allah and Muhammad is the Messenger of Allah', should be the last words said or heard by the dying. The body is washed, wrapped in a shroud and buried – if possible on the same day, with the face turned towards Mecca. Simple prayers are said and the traditional belief is that two angels will soon visit the dead in order to examine the sincerity of the recital of the creed. Chastisement or reward will then begin in the grave, in preparation for the resurrection on the Day of the Judgement. But the Quran says very little about the interim between death and resurrection and the two scholars who have made a careful study of modern expositions of *The Islamic Understanding of Death and Resurrection* (Smith and Haddad, 1981) conclude that 'it is next to impossible to construct anything like a coherent sequence of events'. The whole emphasis is on resurrection and judgement, and there the powerfully vivid imagery of 'the Signs of the Hour' was obviously not intended to be accurate in every detail. What matters is the proclamation of the justice and mercy of God, a message which is open to a variety of interpretations in Islamic thought.

Some similar features can be found in the teaching of Jesus about death and its consequences, for example in the parable where the rich farmer is warned: 'You fool, this very night you must surrender your life' (Luke 12:20). But it is clear that the most urgent part of his message was not about judgement after death, which is not mentioned in the Lord's Prayer (where, most scholars agree, the 'time of trial' from which the disciple prays to be delivered is expected to occur on earth). The proclamation was that 'the time has come; the Kingdom of God is near you; repent and believe the good news' (Mark 1:15).

Jesus and his first followers hoped that the kingdom would 'come' fully in the near future, having already dawned 'on earth', but the date for completion was left to the decision of the Father and the Christians learned that the most important clues to the character of the kingdom were provided by the death and resurrection of Jesus himself: there must be patience and there must be suffering because there must be love, not violence of any sort. (In contrast, at 4:156–7 the Quran denies that Jesus was crucified, since being killed by a death so utterly humiliating was an unthinkable fate for a messenger whom, we are told in 3:45–49, Allah caused to 'ascend' and 'return' to him.) Neither Jesus nor his chief interpreter, Paul, left behind any books of revelations and instructions comparable with the Quran or the *haddith*. In the last analysis of what constitutes authority for Christians, the Word of God is therefore not a book but Jesus himself.

In the Quran the majestic justice of Allah is the key which unlocks the mystery of death. In the New Testament, which looks back to the death and resurrection as well as to the teaching of Jesus, the key is divine love, love which is willing to suffer. What is new in the account of God is the centrality of his love, so astonishingly placarded on the cross which became the supreme symbol of Christianity. What is new in the ethics is the use of love as the consistent test of obedience to the Father. The warnings about the consequences of the rejection of this message are not weak. In Mark's gospel the person who calls a healing demonic cannot receive the forgiveness of the Father until the difference between good and evil has been recognized; the person who nurses comparatively trivial grievances cannot receive that mercy until the need for mercy has been acknowledged; the person who loves life with selfish egotism at the centre will lose life; it would be better if the disciple who betrays Jesus to death had never been born (3:29, 8:35, 11:25, 14:21). But the most solemn warning about the outcome of sin is delivered when Jesus suffers in physical and mental agony; because humanity is full of sin, that is what it costs to deliver the warning and judgement which are God's.

The most vivid picture of life after death in what was reported in the teaching of Jesus comes in Luke's gospel (16:19–31) through the story of the rich man and the poor man; the latter's name, Lazarus, is the Greek version of Eleazar ('Whom God Helps'). The poor man is in Hades, the Greek version of Sheol, and he reclines 'in Abraham's bosom', on a couch during a meal, although neither he nor Abraham has been baptized as a Christian. A 'chasm' is fixed between this feast where the diners are at ease and the 'torment' of the fire which afflicts the rich man, presumably in Gehenna, because the rich man has not been rich in love. Both men and Abraham have bodies, it seems, although the Last Judgement has not arrived. This parable is of course a warning against the ill-treatment of the poor but it demonstrates no confidence in the power of the fear of hell to reform or to deter the unloving. The rich man who is being tormented still expects the poor man to be his servant: 'Abraham, my father, send Lazarus to cool my tongue.' And since the rich man's five brothers, who are leading similarly evil lives, pay no attention to 'the Law and the Prophets' as things are, they would not repent if Lazarus were to be sent to them as a messenger from the land of the dead, as the rich man asks Abraham.

Mark's gospel (9:42–48) shows Jesus using the traditional images of Gehenna, including 'unquenchable fire' and 'the worm that never dies', without any touch of humour, in order to warn against causing children to 'stumble'. It would be more sensible to cut off a foot or a hand, or tear out an eye, than go to Gehenna after an offence so grossly unloving. Gehenna is mentioned ten more times in the other gospels and seven of these references are by Matthew. It is Matthew (18:23–35) who gives us the parable comparing God with an employer who punishes a heartless servant by torture in prison until an immensely large debt has been repaid, which of course cannot be done. The warning about Gehenna is here extended to those who sneer at a 'brother' or look lustfully at a woman (5:22, 28–30). When Pharisees make converts, they make them 'twice as fit for Gehenna' (23:15). At the climax of the great last parable, those who in 'all the nations' have neglected the poor, the sick and the prisoners are led away into the punishment by fire in the age to come (25:41, 46). The message is designed to arouse a healthy fear: 'Fear him who is able to destroy both soul and body in Gehenna' (10:28, with a parallel in Luke 12:4, 5).

If all these warnings in Matthew's gospel were to be taken literally they would suggest a very strange picture of God, for they would suggest that God lacks what humans would regard as common sense, being able to suppose that endless torture would teach the importance of forgiveness and being unable to distinguish between a look and a killing as he distributes punishments. Taken literally, these passages would also raise questions which would destroy their solemnity. How can an unquenchable fire avoid burning up these bodies (as in a crematorium)? How can a worm have endless dinners without destroying the body on which it feasts? But it is common sense to say that Jesus never intended the passages to be taken literally. If he did speak exactly as reported by Matthew (which seems unlikely in view of what is taught elsewhere), he was using traditional imagery, going back to Egypt for the imagery of judgement after death and to Persia for the imagery of the Last Judgement, with both traditions reaching him through post-exilic Judaism. The imagery of 'wailing and grinding of teeth' was, however, not powerful enough for his purpose; in Matthew's gospel this imagery is so lacking in force that at 13:42 people who have been thrown into a blazing furnace carry on gnashing teeth and at 24:51 a man who has been 'cut in pieces' is still able to grind his teeth. And the warnings about missing the wedding or the banquet were also not severe enough. At 22:1–14 Matthew had to add to the story which he shared with Luke two scenes of violence: a battle between the king's messengers and those who reject his invitations (a battle which ends with the whole city being set on fire), and the anger of the king that a guest who had been 'gathered' from the street at the last moment was not wearing a wedding robe and so had to be bound hand and foot and cast into 'the outer darkness'.

In John's gospel as in Paul's letters unbelievers simply 'perish' (3:16) but there is hope that finally 'all' will be drawn by the strange glory of the cross of Jesus (12:32). In a different author's Revelation of John, however, the conflict between the Christian community and its persecutors, already reflected in John's gospel and Matthew's, is dramatized as a cosmic conflict between good and evil, and the images of hell are fiery. There are moments of something approaching optimism (at 5:13 'every created thing' praises God and in chapter 21 the new Jerusalem has to be 1,500 miles wide to accommodate all the saints including 'the kings of the earth'), but the atmosphere is lit by the fires of hell. As early as 2:11 there is a warning about 'the second death'. This is expanded into predictions that those who worship 'the Beast' will be 'tormented in sulphurous flames for ever and ever' (14:10, 11) and that the Devil will join the Beast in the 'lake of fire' (20:10), together with a personified Death and 'any whose names were not to be found in the roll of the living' (20:14, 15).

The Greek name for hell, Tartarus, is found as the fate of sinful angels in a document of about the same date (2 Peter 2:4). It was there that Homer (or whoever added to Homer's work) beheld the punishments for lust, greed and over-ambition which lodged themselves in the imaginations of the ancient world: Tityus eaten by vultures, Tantalus unable to reach the fruit which dangles above him and Sisyphus rolling uphill a stone which promptly rolled downhill. Later Greeks, including Plato, expanded this picture.

Matthew's gospel, the Revelation of John and non-biblical sources are therefore the main suppliers of the imagery in the traditional Christian idea of hell. The imagery was intended to produce horror at the prospect, but even in the New Testament its impact could be softened. In Matthew's gospel (11:23), unbelieving Capernaum is threatened not with Gehenna but with Hades or Sheol, and the punishment of notorious Sodom will be more bearable. (In the still fiercer Letter of Jude the people of Sodom are in Gehenna.) Unfaithful servants will receive beatings which will be severe or light (Luke 12:47, 48). 'People will be forgiven for their sins and whatever blasphemies they utter' (Mark 3:28), either in this age or in the age to come (Matthew 12:32), provided that they do not call evil good, a sin against the Holy Spirit of truth. Above all there was the promise of the dying Jesus to the bandit, who in the end believed that the kingdom would 'come': 'today you shall be with me in Paradise' (Luke 23:43). This total and immediate forgiveness was better than any promise to be spared at the Last Judgement or to be allowed to rest in peace until the day of resurrection.

It could also be believed that after his death 'Christ in the spirit made his proclamation to the spirits in prison' in order that 'in the spirit they might be alive to God' (1 Peter 3:18, 4:6). This belief seems to connect with the story in Matthew's gospel (27:51–53) that 'saints' (presumably heroes and heroines of the Hebrew Bible) were resurrected along with Christ, and from the third century the traditional interpretation was that these were spirits of the dead imprisoned in Hades and delivered by Jesus between his death and his resurrection. Attractively, this interpretation harmonized with the ancient myths about heroic visits to the underworld at which we have already glanced. From the fourth century a tradition in Western Europe, which was to develop into the text known as the Apostles' Creed, taught that Christ *descendit ad infernos*, presumably for this purpose although the phrase may be interpreted as referring to the crucifixion. In the Middle Ages this 'harrowing of hell' (an inaccurate term since Hades was not hell) was often enacted with gusto in amateur dramatics, and was more solemnly interpreted to mean that at least some of the heroes of the Old Testament and some 'good pagans' such as Socrates and Plato had been rescued. In modern times it has been asked: why not Africans, say, or Indians or Chinese? But the original passage did not encourage speculations of this sort, for it said that 'the imprisoned spirits had refused obedience long ago, while God waited patiently in the days of Noah and the building of the ark' (1 Peter 3:20). It seems probable that these 'spirits' were originally thought of either as the exceptionally wicked contemporaries of Noah or as the disobedient angels, 'the sons of the gods' who 'saw that the daughters of men were beautiful' and had sex with them, starting the time of evil which was punished by the Flood (Genesis 6:1–3). In that last case this passage in the Letter of Peter is of interest as contradicting the belief in the Letter of Jude (verse 6) that the disobedient angels are still in prison. And it does not seem possible to clear up the confusion by treating as authoritative the practice of the Christians in Corinth of having themselves baptized a second time, on behalf of the dead (an oddity at which we have already glanced). We are left with the need to think out the question of the eternal destiny of non-Christians from first principles.

So how should this key, love which is willing to suffer, be applied to the idea of hell?

It should not be applied with sentimentality. It must be 'a fearful thing to fall into the hands of the living God' (Hebrews 10:31) – the God who is 'holy, holy, holy, the Lord God Almighty, who was and is and is to come' (Revelation 4:8). As seen from the standpoint of the obstinately evil, God's love is likely to be seen as the justice which punishes: a naughty child sees the correction by a loving and therefore sad parent as punishment, and an adult criminal who surrendered to anger, greed or drugs sees only that the police, the jury and the judge are hostile. Accordingly, the John who wrote the Revelation when acutely aware of the evil in the Roman Empire reported a vision of 'a great white throne and the One who sat on it . . . I could see the dead, both great and small, standing before the throne, and books were opened' (20:11, 12). But the John who wrote the gospel saw more deeply into the relationship between God and human evil: 'this is the judgement: that light has come into the world and people loved darkness rather than light because their deeds were evil' (3:19). This insight is deeper because in John's gospel it is seen that the condemnation of the evil in the world comes when 'the ruler of this world has been condemned' not by a Judge on a throne but by a defenceless man who is 'seen and hated' (15:24, 16:11). When in this gospel Jesus said 'now is the judgement of this world', 'he said this to indicate the kind of death he was to die' (12:31, 33). The condemnation of evil comes in allowing evil to take its course to self-destruction although this policy involves the apparent destruction of the Judge. That seems to be a central insight in John's gospel although some passages (for example 5:28, 29) give the more conventional picture of the Last Judgement after the final resurrection. And it became central in the thought of C. S. Lewis, a resolute interpreter of Christian orthodoxy to the often hellish twentieth century. In *The Problem of Pain* (1940) came the insight which he worked out imaginatively in *The Great Divorce* (1945): 'I willingly believe that the doors of Hell are locked on the inside.'

An emphasis which has become very strong in recent Christian thought is, however, that the suffering and death of Jesus embody the suffering love which the Father always has for his creation and his people – always has and always seeks to reveal. That emphasis agrees with the insistence of Paul that God is best addressed through the '*Abba*, Father' of the prayer which Jesus gave to his disciples (Galatians 4:6, Romans 8:15) and that the Father 'proves his love towards us in that while we were still sinners Christ died for us' (Romans 5:8). Even in the very judgemental Revelation of John, the 'living creatures' who chant praise 'by day and night' around the throne of the Judge see between them and the throne, or in the middle of the throne itself (the Greek could have either meaning) 'a lamb standing as if it had been slaughtered' (4:1 – 5, 6). This lamb is obviously the symbol of Christ in whom 'God was reconciling the world to himself', as Paul wrote in his second surviving letter to Corinth (5:19).

At that crisis the Judge sees that many who sin 'do not know what they are doing': Luke (23:34) has the image of Jesus saying this repeatedly while the nails are being driven through his wrists. And even those who do know what is evil, and who love it, cannot detract from the supreme and irreversible revelation of a love which is nothing less than divine. That glory amid horror 'is accomplished' when Jesus dies, as John's gospel affirms (19:30). In the history of Christianity it has often proved hard to reconcile the image of the Judge with the image of the Saviour. There have been various attempts to solve the problem, ranging from the appeals by medieval fear, to the compassion of the Judge's mother, to the claim which may be found in modern liberalism that the Saviour is totally undiscriminating. But the message of the New Testament is clear, particularly in the testimonies by both Paul and John: the work of Christ is the breakthrough in God's plan for universal salvation and the condemnation is self-inflicted by any who, knowing what they do, refuse to accept what is accomplished.

Human experience can, it seems, be a help in beginning to understand this love which, however, is infinitely greater than any human love. When we love we see what is best in the beloved, and we hope that the relationship will result in what is best in both of us prevailing over the imperfections. But the relationship may be ended by the one who is loved and its end may be tragically destructive. That can be agony for the lover too.

If the end of the relationship with God would mean the self-destruction of a child of God, the tragedy would be of such dimensions that it has often been felt in recent years that God, the Creator and Father whose power and love are infinitely great, would never allow it. And surely it is right – indeed, imperative – to hope that no such tragedy will ever occur. As we have seen, the New Testament expresses that hope very clearly. If we may extend the image used by C. S. Lewis, we must picture God as always hammering for admission on hell's locked doors – always hammering and always ignored. Yet much in the evidence – in the New Testament, in our experience of life – suggests that God puts a value on human freedom which astounds and often dismays us because it goes against our own tendencies to think that power must be domineering and love must be possessive. We think that he must break down the door. But will he?

Luke (13:1–5) tells the story of the response of Jesus to those who believed that some Galileans had been killed by Pilate, and some people in Jerusalem had been killed by a falling tower, because they were greater sinners than anyone else. He dismissed the notion. But he did not pretend that no one is a sinner: 'I tell you, unless you repent, you will all of you come to the same end.' That reply was in tune with the frequent emphasis in the gospels on the unexpected patience of the Father, who appears inactive, who acts only in a way which leaves people free to 'believe' or not, and who will not end the freedom of sinners to perish.

One of the parables tells of the farmer who patiently watches wheat and weeds growing together in his fields, until harvest-time or bonfire-time (Matthew 13:24–30). Another shows how evil is allowed to grow, for it tells of the stupid person who gets rid of an 'unclean spirit' but does not replace it with positive good, so that room is made for seven spirits of evil (Luke 11:24–27). Another tells of tenants who treat messengers from the owner with increasing contempt and so bring about their own destruction (Luke 20:9–19). Another is far more cheerful when it pictures the Father as a shepherd determined to find one lost sheep even if it means leaving the rest of the flock of a hundred. It is even more cheerful when it pictures the joy of the shepherd as he carries the dirty, exhausted and frightened sheep home on his shoulders. But, according to Luke (15:1–7), the parable was told in order to indicate the 'joy in the presence of the angels of God over one sinner who repents'. The implication seems clear: the joy is great because the danger was real, the obstinately stupid sheep could have perished. In the next parable, where the divine Father is compared to a housewife frantically searching in a dark cottage for a lost coin, it seems to be implied that the coin could have remained hidden. And when the Father is compared to a human father who has been insulted by an extremely foolish son, it is clear that the young man has to decide for himself to 'go back to my father'.

Since God's parent-like love is the only possible source of life after death, the possible refusal of that life through a free person's choice of self-destruction seems to be what is permanently, profoundly and fearfully true in the traditional images of hell.

10

Heaven without Another World

IT IS COMPARATIVELY EASY to show that many past beliefs about the immortality of the soul or the resurrection of the body have become incredible once they have been exposed to modern knowledge about the physical basis of personality, in particular about the dependence of 'mind' or 'soul' on an individual's unique and perishable brain and body. It is also comparatively easy to show that many past beliefs about hell are best forgotten. But it is necessary to say positively and clearly what now seems to be true in the idea of heaven. Even in the ages when images of Paradise were multiplied, as if the Garden of Eden had got out of control, there was always in the minds of thoughtful people a hesitation. Paul's first letter to Corinth had near its beginning (at 2:9) a quotation about the heavenly things. 'No eye has seen them, no ear has heard them, no heart has imagined them, but they have been prepared by God for those who love him.' It is typical of our uncertainty that we do not know the source of Paul's quotation: Origen thought it came from the Revelation of Elijah, which has been lost because in the end it was not accepted by Jews or Christians as Scripture.

The Revelation of John (20:4–6) included the idea that the martyrs would be resurrected physically and would reign on earth 'with Christ for a thousand years', an idea which has fascinated many Christians, including many who have not been eager for martyrdom. But the final vision of John was of a new start with 'a new heaven and a new earth'. In earlier chapters John had pictured heaven as a temple, a picture which has encouraged many clergy and monks to hope that their services will always be required, but in the city made of gold in that final vision, 'I saw no temple, for its temple was the sovereign Lord God and the Lamb' (21:22).

Paul's contemporary Philo of Alexandria dismissed the idea that the dead can live in the *aether*, maintaining that outside the universe 'there is no place but God'. That thought did not prevent talk by the more imaginative about seven heavens. It is possible to trace the growth of medieval ideas and images about the 'empyrean' where reality is in the form of the 'quintessence'. The sublime poem of Dante included fourteenth-century space travel as it left the 'earthly paradise' for higher realms. But since then actual expeditions to the planets, and observations through giant telescopes, have not encouraged such speculations. The image of angels playing harps on clouds has become comic.

Early in the Middle Ages an Irish saint, Brendan, dreamed of crossing the Atlantic to settle in the Isles of the Blessed, but when he landed he found that he was not allowed to explore very far: so to speak, he lacked a visa because he was not dead. During the Middle Ages almost all the Christian dead were entrusted to God by being buried in unmarked graves in the churchyard: then, in a process gathering pace from the Renaissance onwards, the centre in hopes of heaven shifted to the continuity of family life and to activities which would be less boring than an uninterrupted singing of hymns. But in the twentieth century, in lands which had been Christian, the breakdown of family life before death has become a frequent feature of 'progress' and most people have not been accustomed to singing hymns, so that pictures of heaven have once again become blurred, when they can be seen at all.

Spiritualists have claimed that pleasant images are communicated to mediums by the dead but it has been widely felt that, if these pictures did originate in the 'afterlife', they were like unexciting photographs of other people's domestic lives in a suburb. Some reports from what some Spiritualists have called 'Summerland' say that it is so familiar that at first the dead do not realize that they have died. That, however, does not seem a real possibility to those who have begun to think seriously. If beyond death there can be no time or space as we know it, dying must mean the end of all projects which needed to be completed within the boundaries of the available time and space. Since in eternity there can be no time to be measured by our normal methods, there can be no timing of development. The life which means Becoming has been replaced by the life which means Being, and that does not take time: it takes eternity. Because there can be no space to be seen or touched, there can be no pleasures or pain derived from seeing or touching: the life which means pleasure or pain has been replaced by the life which means unchanging joy.

Any idea of an 'other world' is therefore liable to mislead. At the end of prayers it used to be a custom to say 'world without end' when heaven was meant, but every world must end and so eternity cannot be a world. We have been given enough worlds in time and space: so far they have taken at least ten (perhaps fifteen) thousand million years to evolve; and light, travelling at 186,282 miles per second, would take at least ten thousand million light-years to cross the universe which includes them and appears to be expanding very fast. What were traditionally called 'the heavens' provide worlds enough for our powers of wonder and imagination, but 'heaven' is utterly different, and we who use the English language are fortunate in that it enables us to distinguish between the 'heavens above' and 'heaven' as the ultimate reality which gave and gives existence to our universe and to whatever other (perhaps larger and older) universes there may be. 'Our Father in heaven' does not mean that an old man looks down on us benevolently but distantly from above the clouds. It means that the Source of all existence is motivated by love – which is our one good reason for hoping that our apparently insignificant and yet total deaths will not be completely the end.

The beliefs which make sense to me as I try to sum up what has been positive in this book are these. When we die we go not to the stars, not to Summerland, not to fairyland and not to any 'other world', but to God, without end. (That is, we go unless we ourselves make the final refusal which brings down on us the judgement which means non-existence – a complete non-existence, without any of the positive and attractive elements in the Buddhist's Nirvana.) And when we live after death that life will not be the immortality of the individual's soul with little change, for such a survival without renewal would indeed bring boredom as we simply carry on being ourselves. Nor will eternity bring the reassembly of our present flesh and bones with improvements, for that kind of resurrection would mean the total reversal (not the mere 'transformation' or 'redemption') of all the laws of the creation which has so marvellously given us the bodies we have before death. Nor will the life which is 'life indeed' be absorption into God or Nature, for that future would not rescue from death what has been of value in the individual's life before death. The most reliable hope seems to be that 'our Father in heaven' will not swallow us, any more than we shall be kept as we are and at a distance. We shall be embraced – embraced by What and Who is reality more real than anything or anyone known by us previously.

For those who are willing to be embraced, the change made when time is replaced by eternity, and space by the glory of God, will be 'purgatory' in the sense that it will purge us. It will liberate us from everything which is unfit to share that final glory. We shall be changed. And in heaven we shall 'praise' because that eternal life will be the fulfilment of all those times before death when we have not looked at our watches while enjoying the sheer delight of being with the people we love most, or being caught up in the rapture of seeing or hearing beauty. Augustine sometimes let his enthusiasm about being with God lead him into speculations which are liable to sound unworthy of a very great teacher, as we have noted in this book, but he wrote some words which combine simplicity with inexhaustible meaning: 'There we shall rest and see, we shall see and love, we shall love and praise.' We shall 'rest': the busy and fretting ego, usually self-serving but often worried, often frustrated and often suffering, will be no more. We shall 'see': the restless search for certainty will be over and all eternity will be needed to appreciate what we see. We shall 'love': all the distances, disappointments, separations and enmities will be replaced by the never-ending union. And therefore we shall 'praise'.

It seems that the individual can survive the body's death only if the Creator continues to love the personality of the human to the extent of replacing the body which was its basis with a new basis: himself in his eternal life. Irenaeus, the bishop and theologian who died in 107, was chiefly concerned to defend the importance of the straightforwardly physical body before death, and was therefore willing to be less cautious than Paul in saying that the dead would have 'bodies', but the spiritual emphasis came out in his teaching that 'those who see God are within God, sharing his glory'. In *The Logic of Perfection* (1962) Charles Hartshorne suggested that 'we can interpret heaven as the conception which God forms of our actual being, a conception which we partly determine by our free decisions but which is more than all our decisions and experiences, since it is the synthesis of God's participatory response to these experiences'. Hartshorne's philosophy has been criticized by some because its language is not biblical, particularly because it is not the language of love, and it seems to be true that only the love which the eternal God has for his creatures can make the idea of eternal life 'with' or 'in' God different from the idea of absorption into Nature or the Infinite. But 'the conception which God forms of our actual being' is a philosopher's way of expressing the religious insight that the Creator holds us in being and 'the synthesis of God's participatory response' is a cool way of speaking about love. It therefore seems right to concentrate on Christian, or potentially Christian, elements in a philosophical system such as Hartshorne's, rather than on elements which are not so easy for Christians to adopt. And if Christ is allowed to define Christianity, a complete concentration on the power of God's love cannot be wrong. Hartshorne wrote that 'not *our* personality is this necessary, this primary, personal unity, but only God's. It is a hard lesson to learn – that God is more important than we are.' And on that point Hartshorne could have quoted Scripture: William Strawson demonstrated in *Jesus and the Future Life* (1970) that 'in the thought of Jesus assurance about the future life arises from the nature of God, not from any other authority; nor firstly from a consideration of human hopes and needs'.

Hartshorne's conviction that individuals can be valued and therefore remembered by God differed very significantly from the philosophy of Alfred North Whitehead, a thinker to whom he owed much.

Whitehead was the founder of 'process' philosophy. With a background of outstanding work in mathematics, he had a religious temperament and expounded a vision of the universe as a single process influenced, rather than controlled, by God. He believed that this limited influence had been chosen by a Creator who had renounced the untroubled divinity of his 'primordial' nature. But because he expressed himself in his own strange terminology when writing formally, it was not easy to tell what he really thought about popular religion, in particular about popular images of hell and heaven. For such information we have to turn to some of his conversations in old age which were recorded by a journalist, Lucien Page. It turns out that in private the philosopher was frankly contemptuous about hell, saying that after the more enlightened teaching of Jesus 'the old ferocious God is back, the Oriental despot, the Pharaoh, the Hitler, with everything to enforce obedience, from infant damnation to eternal punishment', in an 'abyss of horror'. Whitehead also thought it 'appallingly idiotic' to insult God by thinking him 'capable of creating angels and men to sing his praises day and night to all eternity'. Such a despot of heaven would be guilty of 'inane and barbaric vanity'. Shortly before his death in 1947 he stated what he positively believed. He told Lucien Page: 'In so far as man partakes of this creative process does he partake of the divine, of God, and participation is his immortality, reducing the question of whether his individuality survives the death of the body to the state of an irrelevancy.'

Many Christians would nowadays agree with Whitehead's rejection of crude images of hell and heaven. But it is harder to agree with the belief which he put in their place, for it exaggerates the creativity which is possible for puny, fragile and mortal humans. While rejecting any idea that God is a despot who enjoys cruelty and demands flattery, this distinguished philosopher (perhaps unduly influenced by the political climate of democracy) flattered us. The sober truth seems to be that when humanity is creative it is more or less Godlike, but no human achievement can make what we do divine. Sceptics as well as believers can agree that if anyone who is dead can be saved from dying completely, an astounding intervention is needed from the power that made, and makes, the universe – although of course many people with fine characters and good minds think such a miracle impossible, so that eternity must for ever remain 'above', not after, human life. It is therefore the faith (no more and no less than faith) of the Jewish, Christian and Islamic religions that the only thing which matters in our end is the immortal power of God. Believers turn to God the supreme, God the merciful, the God who can lead us through the valley of death. God can save us after our deaths somewhat as ants can be picked up by people – or so it is believed.

Obviously life is often good for us, but it is equally clear that the problem of evil challenges belief in God. The main use made of Whitehead's philosophy by Christian theologians has therefore been accepting it as a reminder from science that much in the 'process' is hard to reconcile – or even to connect – with the concept of God as both supremely powerful and supremely loving. No easy intellectual answer has ever been produced to this very painfully familiar question but at least it is certain that, if after our deaths the supremacy of the parent-like God is demonstrated by our experience of being rescued, it cannot be 'inane and barbaric' if something a bit like a song is raised. The author of a scholarly *History of Heaven* (1997), Jeffery Burton Russell, concluded that heaven is 'the song which God sings to us' – so to speak, a song of triumph celebrating the completion of creative labour. That must come first. But in the same metaphorical sense we may also say that those who have been plucked from total death would find it very sensible to join that divine song, reaching beyond music.

Dante had one of the most fertile imaginations in the history of literature but his greatest triumph came at the end of his *Paradiso* when he was eloquent about the failure of all words and images to reach far enough. What he saw was Light, one Light. There was more than one intensity of Light because this was not only the Source of all existence but also Love, binding it all together 'as pages are bound in a book'. The Light blazed as Love, 'the love which moves the sun and the other stars' and which draws humans to this fulfilment. And in the intensity of Light as Love could be seen a human figure, who could only have one human name.

It was because of his trust in the Father who cannot die that Jesus taught 'the resurrection of the dead'. And, on this basis, what he taught and did can provide a sufficient assurance, even during the constant uncertainty which is the human response to the mystery of death. The early Christians knew very well that any 'resting places' after death would have to be in the one 'house' of God the Father, and they were confident that they would find there the Lord they already knew (John 14:1–4). They knew very well that 'God alone possesses immortality, dwelling in unapproachable light' (1 Timothy 1:16) and they were confident that this true God had 'broken the power of death and brought life and immortality to light through the good news' (2 Timothy 1:10). This was the news which Paul accepted and communicated when he became 'convinced that nothing in life or death . . . can separate us from the love of God in Christ Jesus our Lord' (Romans 8:39). In a moment when the prophet Hosea had thought that God lacked compassion, he had pictured him summoning death with its poisonous 'sting' to punish and destroy his enemies (13:14). Now Paul cried out in victory: 'Death, where is your sting?' (1 Corinthians 15:55). And despite his fear that some might reject the glory of God to the end, he was one of the great optimists, writing in his first letter to Corinth that finally 'God will be all in all' (15:28) and quoting to the Philippians (2:10, 11) the hope in the hymn that:

> at the name of Jesus every knee shall bow,
> in heaven, on earth, in the depths,
> and every tongue say 'Jesus Christ is Lord'
> to the glory of God the Father.

The gospel of John is as confident as the letters of Paul in this triumph over death. Naturally, many readers now ask critical questions about the way in which John expressed his faith. There are historical questions, including: was Lazarus really freed from his tomb (the other gospels do not mention it); did Jesus really speak on his last evening the long discourse and prayer which this gospel (only) includes? Or is that story about Lazarus a great myth or drama proclaiming the real conquest of death by life? And are the words of farewell pure gold because they have been refined by many years of experience that the Jesus who died really is able to be with his disciples in life and in death, giving a peace which no one and nothing can take away? We miss noticing great spiritual wealth if we do not see that behind this strange gospel is the experience that 'this is eternal life: to know you, the only true God, and Jesus Christ whom you have sent' (17:3). It is not literally true that the believing disciple 'will never die' (8:51, 11:26), and the impression that this was meant literally has to be corrected (21:23), but solid experience is the foundation of the faith that the believer already 'has' eternal life (5:24), so that those who believe in Jesus, even though they die, will live (11:25). The community behind this gospel believes that 'those who do the will of God will live for ever' because 'we know that we have already passed from death to life' (1 John 2:17, 3:14).

Because Christians have already been given this intense experience of a life which reaches above and beyond death – because in present experience 'whoever has the Son has life and whoever does not have the Son of God does not have life' (1 John 5:12) – it does not follow that 'only orthodox Christians ever go to heaven'. The sayings of Jesus which the first three gospels preserve (with editorial arrangements and touches) include no such teaching. It is indeed said, very urgently, that 'the gate which leads to life is narrow and the road is hard, and few find it' (Matthew 7:14). So at any cost the hearer must 'struggle to get in through the narrow door' (Luke 13:24). But many are invited to the feast on the other side of the door and as he seeks guests the Father finds anyone who is willing to be found. According to the sayings of Jesus two essentially simple things are necessary, and only two, and they arise from the two essential commandments. Those who in their hearts want God will see him; those who in their actions love their neighbours will see the reward he gives (Matthew 5:3–8, 8:11). Matthew's gospel is, as we have seen, the most sternly judgmental of all the four – but it ends its presentation of the teaching of Jesus with the vision of 'all the nations' being judged according to their practice of charity. Those who care for the hungry, the lonely, the destitute, the sick and the imprisoned are told: 'Come, you who are blessed by my Father, inherit the kingdom prepared for you from the foundation of the world' (25:34).

But no promises are made to people who would not be satisfied with what is on offer. It would be foolish to invest one's life thinking that the profit will be in things which can become rusty or moth-eaten (Matthew 6:19, 20). Nothing is promised to people whose only interest in heaven is in the continuation of family life or any other of the great pleasures of life before death. Because the Father is parent-like, he can be expected to support with his own being all that is good as a result of arrangements on earth – on the earth which he created – but the arrangements in the 'age to come' can no longer be physical or exclusive. This means that they must be transformed into a share in the eternal and all-embracing Father's love and bliss. That alone is what satisfies and lasts. Realism about heaven which makes every hope hang on the reality of God is summed up in some of the Christian Bible's most daring words, that people who at present know 'the corruption that is in the world because of lust' may become 'participants in the divine nature' (2 Peter 1:4).

Mark (12:18–25) recorded the most important statement of Jesus about life after death, made when he knew that his own death was near and when he was being questioned by Sadducees 'who say that there is no resurrection'. Attempting to trap him into teaching what was not biblical, they gave the ridiculous example of a woman who in obedience to the Law of Moses was married to seven short-lived brothers in turn, in the hope of having children: to the Sadducees, children were the one possibility of immortality of a kind. 'At the resurrection, when they come back to life' – or so it is said – 'whose wife will she be?' Jesus replied that although the Sadducees proudly claimed that their own authority was based on the authority of the Bible, they did not understand the real message of the Scriptures because they did not understand the character of the power of God, exercised chiefly in showing mercy and love.

Jesus taught that people 'rise from the dead' simply because God will not forsake them. He permanently 'is' the God of Abraham, Isaac and Jacob, who with 'all the prophets' (Luke 13:28) and with 'many from east and west will come to feast in the kingdom of heaven' (Matthew 8:11). The many will include obscure and unfortunate people like the woman in a story which, while no doubt intended to be comic, reflects a society where a woman could be passed from man to man as a breeding machine. But Jesus said nothing to suggest that after her death the woman would be given a new body or would need one. He also said nothing to suggest that her marriage to one of the brothers would be made truly permanent. Marriage is by its very nature both physical and exclusive: the down-to-earth basis is essential to the possibility that it will become the most intense and the most joyful of all human relationships, but that basis must end with a partner's death. What Jesus offered was a relationship in 'the age to come', which would never end. It would be better than any happy marriage, which meant being desirable beyond words. It would be a relationship with the God who is 'not the God of the dead but of the living', the God who gives life with all its goodness before death and after it; and through that relationship there would also be the relationship with others which would come to be called the 'communion of saints', for what Jesus was speaking about could be thought of as a banquet and properly a banquet is a scene of close and delighted fellowship. 'When they rise from the dead men and women do not marry; they are like angels in heaven.' In other words, they are purely spiritual and their relationships with God and with each other include no cloud of misunderstanding or separation. By presenting the eternal Creator as 'Father', Jesus surely implied that in eternity what is good in parenthood is transcended, not lost, and that must also be true of marriage, but the 'good news' brought by Jesus was not about family life or marriage going on for ever: it was about God, about 'glory' meaning perfection and about a future of glory because of God. That is the future to which the best of marriages or of families is only an introduction.

Matthew says that 'the people were astounded at this teaching', presumably because it was so magnificently simple as the end to a very long search and to many speculations and disagreements. Luke, explaining that this teaching was the good news that 'for God all are alive', added a comment by an unusual expert on the religious laws which include some in God's blessing and exclude others: 'Well spoken!' (20:39). And so the death of Jesus himself could be understood through these simple words: '*Abba*, Father, into your hands I commit my spirit' (23:46).

Some Books

THIS IS NO MORE THAN a selection of studies, most of them recent and more technical than this book. Where possible, the British publishers of the latest editions or printings are listed so dates may differ from those of the first editions mentioned in the text.

Chapter 1 WHERE WE ARE

Henry Scott Holland's sermon is in his *Facts of Faith* (Longmans, 1919). Steven Pinker expounded *How the Mind Works* (Allen Lane, 1997). Simon Blackburn compiled *The Oxford Dictionary of Philosophy* (Oxford University Press, 1994). Paul Tillich, *The Eternal Now* (SCM Press, 1963), and Milton McGatch, *Death: Meaning and Morality in Contemporary Christian Culture* (Allen and Unwin, 1969), rejected personal survival. D. Z. Phillips and Timothy Tessin edited *Religion without Transcendence?* (Macmillan, 1997) but the best presentation of a non-realist view of God remains Stewart Sutherland, *God, Jesus and Belief* (Blackwell, 1984). Nicholas Lash interpreted the Apostles' Creed in *Believing Three Ways in One God* (SCM Press, 1992) but the high quality of his teaching is shown more fully by his *The Beginning and the End of 'Religion'* (Cambridge University Press, 1996). Peter Berger, *The Social Reality of Religion* (Faber and Faber, 1967), and John Bowker, *The Meanings of Death* (Cambridge University Press, 1993), were studies of outstanding value. Frank Reynolds and Earle Waugh edited *Religious Encounters with Death* (Pennsylvania State University Press, 1977).

Chapter 2 DEATH'S CHANGING FACE

After a period when Geoffrey Gorer could complain about casualness in *Death, Grief and Mourning in Contemporary Britain* (Cresset, 1965), Tony Walter noted *The Revival of Death* (Routledge, 1994), accompanied by *The Eclipse of Eternity* (Macmillan, 1996). Peter Jupp and Tony Rogers edited essays on theology and pastoral practice in *Interpreting Death* (Cassell, 1997) and Glennys Howarth and Peter Jupp edited *Contemporary Issues in the Sociology of Death and Dying* and *The Changing Face of Death* (Macmillan, 1996, 1997). Michael Kearl, *Endings* (Oxford University Press, 1989), was mainly about death in the USA, and Marilyn Webb, *The Good Death* (Bantam Books, 1997), was a guide to 'the new American search to reshape the end of life'. James Farrell traced the history of *Inventing the American Way of Death, 1830–1920* (Temple University Press, 1980). D. C. Sloane explored American cemeteries in *The Last Great Necessity* (John Hopkins University Press, 1991). David Clark edited essays on *The Sociology of Death* (Blackwell, 1993), and Jon Davies on *Ritual and Remembrance* (Sheffield University Press, 1994). Douglas Davies gave one sociologist's overview of *Death, Ritual and Belief* (Cassell, 1997). Elisabeth Kübler-Ross, *On Death and Dying* (Tavistock-Routledge, 1973), raised awareness.

The foremost histories of attitudes to death AD are Philippe Ariès, *The Hour of Our Death* (Oxford University Press, 1991), John McManners, *Death and the Enlightenment* (Oxford University Press, 1985), and Michel Vovelle, *La Mort et l'Occident de 1300 à Nos Jours* (Gallimard, Paris, 1981). These are mainly about France, as is Thomas Kselman, *Death and the Afterlife in Modern France* (Princeton University Press, 1993). T. S. R. Boase introduced *Death in the Middle Ages* (Thames and Hudson, 1972) and Frederick Paxton studied the earlier *Christianizing Death: The Creation of a Ritual Process in Early Modern Europe* (Cornell University Press, 1990). Studies of English history include Eamon Duffy, *The Stripping of the Altars: Traditional Religion in England c.1400–c.1580* (Yale University Press, 1992), Clare Gittings, *Death, Burial and the Individual in Early Modern England* (Croom Helm, 1984), Julian Little, *The English Way of Death: The Common Funeral Service Since 1450* (Robert Hale, 1991) and Michael Wheeler, *Death and the Future Life in Victorian Literature and Theology* (Cambridge University Press, 1990). Jonathan Dollimore, *Death, Desire and Loss in Western Culture* (Allen Lane, 1998), is mainly about the twentieth century. Sarah Goodwin and Elisabeth Bronfen edited *Death and Representation* (John Hopkins University Press, 1993).

Philippe Ariès also wrote the text of *Images of Man and Death* (Harvard University Press, 1985) and *Western Attitudes toward Death* (Marion Boyars, 1994), and contributed to *Death in America* edited by David Stannard (University of Pennsylvania Press, 1976).

A readable introduction to anthropology in this field is Nigel Barclay, *Dancing on the Grave* (Abacus, 1995). The Cambridge University Press published the study of *Celebrations of Death* by Richard Huntington and Peter Metcalf (1991) and the essays on *Death and the Regeneration of Life* edited by Maurice Bloch and Jonathan Parry (1982). Maurice Bloch explored the 'politics of religious experience' in *Prey into Hunter* (Cambridge University Press, 1992). J. S. Curl, *A Celebration of Death* (Batsford, 1993), was architectural.

Chapter 3 WHY WE ASK

D. J. Enright edited two literary anthologies, *The Oxford Book of Death* and *The Oxford Book of the Supernatural* (Oxford University Press, 1987, 1994). Piero Prioreschi provided a *History of Human Responses to Death* (Edwin Mellen Press, 1990). Jacques Choron summed up the history of philosophers' responses in *Death and Western Man* (Collier Macmillan, 1973) and John Fischer edited essays on *The Metaphysics of Death* (Stanford University Press, 1993). John Carse concluded *Death and Existence* (John Wiley, New York, 1980) with the thought that the meaning lies in 'the attempt to embrace the incomprehensibility of death' and Ernest Becker discussed *The Denial of Death* (Collier Macmillan, 1973). But a surgeon, Sherwin Nuland, was comprehensible about *How We Die* (Random House, 1997). Marcia Colish is the best historian of *The Stoic Tradition* (in two volumes, Brill, Leiden, 1990) and J. M. C. Toynbee of *Death and Burial in the Roman World* (Thames and Hudson, 1971). Studies of myths include Alexander Heidel, *The Gilgamesh Epic and Old Testament Parallels* (University of Chicago Press, 1946). A. J. Spencer expertly introduced *Death in Ancient Egypt* (Penguin Books, 1991) and H. R. E. Davidson *Scandinavian Mythology* (Hamlyn, 1982).

Interesting collections of essays include *Death and the Afterlife* edited by Stephen Davis and *Beyond Death* edited by Dan Cohn-Sherbok and Christopher Lewis (Macmillan, 1989, 1995), with *Reflections on Death* by Jews edited by Jack Riemer (Shocken Books, New York, 1994).

Chapter 4 A MODERN SEARCH

R. W. K. Paterson, *Philosophy and Belief in Life after Death* (Macmillan, 1995), turned for illumination to parapsychology, a difficult subject surveyed by John Beloff, *Parapsychology: A Concise History* (Athlone Press, 1993), and Anthony North, *The Paranormal* (Cassell: Blandford, 1997). In *Wings of Illusion* (Polity Press, 1990) John Schumaker, and in *Soul Searching* (Chatto and Windus, 1995) Nicholas Humphrey, thought it all nonsense. Lee Bailey and Jenny Yates edited recent material, including science-based explanation, about *The Near Death Experience* (Routledge, 1996) and Ian Watson, *Life after Death?: The Evidence* (Macmillan, 1997), was more anecdotal. R. C. Finucane, *Appearances of the Dead* (Junction Books, 1982), was 'a cultural history of ghosts' and Gillian Bennett, *Traditions of Belief* (Penguin Books, 1987), was a reminder that the history has not stopped. Carol Zaleski compared modern with earlier accounts of *Otherworld Journeys* (Oxford University Press, New York, 1987). The accounts which started the recent discussion are in Raymond Moody, *Life after Life* (Bantam, 1975).

Chapter 5 TRADITIONS

Geoffrey Rowell provided a history of *The Liturgy of Christian Burial* (SPCK, 1977). My *What is Catholicism?* (Cassell: Mowbray, 1994) responded to the *Catechism of the Catholic Church* (Cassell: Geoffrey Chapman, 1994). I have offered a larger history of *Christianity: The First Two Thousand Years*, now a paperback (Cassell, 1998). The Book of Common Prayer may be contrasted with *The Puritan Way of Death* as studied by David Stannard (Oxford University Press, 1977).

Chapter 6 REAL POSSIBILITIES

Paul Badham, *Christian Beliefs about Life after Death* (Macmillan, 1994), is a clear introduction, as is Hans Küng, *Eternal Life?* (Collins, 1984), but of course from a German background. Good short books by other theologians include John Macquarrie's (Mowbray, 1978) and Brian Hebblethwaite's (Marshall, Morgan and Scott, 1984), the one more philosophical, the other more historical but both called *The Christian Hope*. Macquarrie's Gifford Lectures, *In Search of Humanity* and *In Search of Deity* (SCM Press, 1982–84), were magisterial. Ray Anderson also discussed *Theology, Death and Dying* (Blackwell, 1986) with a largely American bibliography. Paul Fiddes, *The Creative Suffering of God* (Oxford University Press, 1988), is the best theological work on that mystery but is appropriately difficult. Its central argument was expressed pastorally by William Vanstone, *Love's Endeavour, Love's Expense* (Darton, Longman and Todd, 1977). One of the best recent books on religion and science was Angela Tilby's *Science and the Soul* (SPCK, 1994) and see the next section.

Chapter 7 ARE SOULS IMMORTAL?

Terence Penelhum formulated problems about *Survival and Disembodied Existence* (Routledge, 1970). Antony Flew, *The Logic of Mortality* (Blackwell, 1987), was a vigorous refutation of Plato and Descartes and David Bostock, *Plato's Phaedo* (Oxford University Press, 1986), a more detailed critique. Robert Garland, *The Greek Way of Death* (Cornell University Press, 1985), and Walter Burkert, *Greek Religion: Archaic and Classical* (Blackwell, 1985), updated Edwin Rhode's *Psyche*, still valuable although first published in 1894 (Ares Publishers, Chicago, 1987).

R. C. Zaehner edited *The Bhagavad Gita* (Oxford University Press, 1994) and W. Y. Evans-Wentz *The Tibetan Book of the Dead* (Oxford University Press, 1960). The Dalai Lama recommended Sogyul Rinpoche, *The Tibetan Book of Living and Dying* (Rider, 1992). Christine Longaker's interpretation is in *Facing Death and Finding Hope* (Arrow Books, 1998) and Francis Cook's is among the essays in *Death and the Afterlife* (Macmillan, 1989) (see Section 3). Jonathan Parry studied Hindu funerary customs in *Death in Banaras* (Cambridge University Press, 1994). Piers Vitebsky, *Dialogues with the Dead* (Cambridge University Press, 1994), studied emotional realities in India.

Francis Crick, *The Astonishing Hypothesis: The Scientific Search for the Soul* (Touchstone, 1995), seems to be partly authoritative and partly provocative. Steven Jones introduced genetics in *In the Blood* (HarperCollins, 1996) and Susan Greenfield brain science in *The Human Brain* (Weidenfeld and Nicolson, 1997). Sir Walter Bodmer and Robin McKie explained the history and uses of genetic research in *The Book of Man* (Abacus, 1995). Richard Gregory wrote a history of *Mind in Science* (Penguin Books, 1993) and William Lycan edited a more technical collection of material in *Mind and Cognition* (Blackwell, 1996). But H. D. Lewis, *Immortality and the Soul* (Macmillan, 1973), and Richard Swinburne, *The Evolution of the Soul* (Oxford University Press, 1986), defended dualism vigorously. The philosopher Sir Karl Popper and the neuroscientist Sir John Eccles were rather more cautious dualists in

The Self and the Brain (Springer International, 1977). John Cooper, *Body, Soul and the Life Everlasting* (Eerdmans, Grand Rapids, 1989), was mainly biblical, and David Braine, *The Human Person: Animal and Spirit* (University of Notre Dame Press, 1992), mainly philosophical. Anthony Hear criticized the reductionism of some biologists in *Beyond Evolution* (Oxford University Press, 1997). Simon Tugwell, *Human Immortality and the Redemption of Death* (SCM Press, 1990), was a scholar's tour of history. In *Being a Person* (Hodder and Stoughton, 1998), John Habgood was a wise guide in a territory where faith and science met.

Chapter 8 ARE BODIES RAISED?

John Hick's *Death and Eternal Life* was reissued in 1985 (Macmillan) and like John Polkinghorne's *Belief in God in an Age of Science* (Yale University Press, 1998) and Keith Ward's *God, Faith and the New Millennium* (Oneworld, 1998) belonged to a series of helpful books by the same author. Caroline Walker Bynum studied *The Resurrection of the Body in Western Christianity 200–1336* (Columbia University Press, 1995) and Piero Camporesi was more interested in folklore in *The Incorruptible Flesh* (Cambridge University Press, 1988). Recent studies of the Hebrew Bible have included James Barr, *The Garden of Eden and the Hope of Immortality* (SCM Press, 1992). Mary Boyce described beliefs of *The Zoroastrians* (Routledge, 1979). George Nickelsburg stressed diversity but gave a clear account of *Resurrection, Immortality and Eternal Life in Inter-Testamental Judaism* (Harvard University Press, 1972). Christopher Rowland, *The Open Heaven* (1982), was a study of the apocalyptic literature in Judaism and early Christianity. Louis Jacobs discussed *Principles of the Jewish Faith* in the light of history (Jason Aronson, 1988) and Dan Cohn-Sherbok presented the variety in *Modern Judaism* (Macmillan, 1996). John Mason studied *The Resurrection according to Paul* (Mullen Biblical Press, 1993). James Dunn, *The Theology of Paul the Apostle* (T. and T. Clark, 1998), was an invaluable synthesis and Andrew Lincoln, *Paradise Now and Not Yet* (Cambridge University Press, 1981), was a more technical study of Pauline eschatology. E. P. Sanders studied the background to Jesus and Paul in *Judaism: Practice and Belief 63 BCE–66 CE* (CSM Press, 1992).

The best recent critical discussions of the resurrection of Jesus are Peter Carnley, *The Structure of Resurrection Belief* (Oxford

University Press, 1987), and Gerd Lüdemann's more sceptical but still Christian *The Resurrection of Jesus* (SCM Press, 1994). Herman Hendrickx, *Resurrection Narratives* (Geoffrey Chapman, 1984), was a critical study by a Roman Catholic scholar. But less difficult studies with more conservative conclusions have also not lacked integrity, notably Murray Harris, *Raised Immortal* (Marshall, Morgan and Scott, 1983), Pheme Perkins, *Resurrection* (Geoffrey Chapman, 1984), and Gerald O'Collins, *Jesus Risen* (Darton, Longman and Todd, 1986). Collections of scholarly essays from different viewpoints include *The Resurrection of Jesus Christ* edited by Paul Avis (Darton, Longman and Todd, 1993), *Resurrection* edited by Stephen Barton and Graham Stanton (SPCK, 1994), *Resurrection Reconsidered* edited by Gavin D'Costa (Oneworld, 1996) and *The Resurrection* edited by Stephen Davis and others (Oxford University Press, 1997). Stephen Davis is the author of *Risen Indeed* (SPCK, 1993).

While this debate continues, William Strawson, *Jesus and the Future Life* (Epworth Press, 1970), has not lost its value. Brian Daley, *The Hope of the Early Church* (Cambridge University Press, 1991), was a history of many developments.

Chapter 9 HELL AS LOVE

The 1728 sermon by Jonathan Edwards is in Volume 14 of his *Sermons and Discourses* edited by Kenneth Ninkesha (Yale University Press, 1997). Alice Turner provided an illustrated *History of Hell* (Hale, 1995), but S. G. F. Brandon, *The Judgement of the Dead* (Weidenfeld and Nicolson, 1967), and J. Gwyn Griffiths, *The Divine Verdict* (Brill, Leiden, 1991), were more serious studies. Jane Smith and Yvonne Haddad presented *The Islamic Understanding of Death and Resurrection* (State University of New York Press, 1981). Gai Eaton, *Islam and the Destiny of Man* (Islamic Texts Society, 1997), was a British Muslim's exposition of that way of life and death.

Alan Bernstein, *The Formation of Hell* (UCL Press, 1993), explored death and retribution in the ancient and early Christian worlds. Martha Himmelfarb recounted *Tours of Hell* (University of Pennsylvania Press, 1983) and Piero Camporesi assembled evidence about *The Fear of Hell* mainly in Catholic countries (Polity Press, 1990). The fall of hell in England was traced by David Walker, *The Decline of Hell* (University of Chicago Press, 1964),

Philip Almond, *Heaven and Hell in Enlightenment England* (Cambridge University Press, 1994), and Geoffrey Rowell, *Hell and the Victorians* (Oxford University Press, 1974).

Stephen Travis discussed the New Testament in *Christ and the Judgement of God* (Marshall, Morgan and Scott, 1986). Jonathan Kvanvig brought a philosopher's mind to *The Problem of Hell* (Oxford University Press, 1993). He concluded that some might choose to live in hell, but John Blanchard was more robust about damnation in *Whatever Happened to Hell?* (Evangelical Press, 1993). John Wenham discussed Evangelical attitudes in *Facing Hell* (Paternoster Press, 1998). Jacques Le Goff, *The Birth of Purgatory* (Scolar Press, 1990), is the authoritative account and J. A. McCulloch, *The Harrowing of Hell* (T. and T. Clark, 1930), was a study of that popular belief. In *The Persistence of Purgatory* (Cambridge University Press, 1995) Richard Fenn argued that the myth has continued to influence the modern world in valuing time.

Chapter 10 HEAVEN WITHOUT ANOTHER WORLD

There are three recent histories of the idea: Ulrich Simon, *Heaven in the Christian Tradition* (Barrie and Rockliff, 1958), the more sociological Colleen McDannell and Bernhard Lang, *Heaven: A History* (Yale University Press, 1988), and the more spiritual Jeffrey Burton Russell, *A History of Heaven* up to Dante (Princeton University Press, 1997). Ulrich Simon mapped many paths taken in *The Ascent to Heaven* (Barrie and Rockliff, 1961) and Martha Himmelfarb studied *Ascent to Heaven in Jewish and Christian Apocalypses* in more detail (Oxford University Press, 1993). Lucien Price edited *Dialogues of Alfred North Whitehead* (North American Library, 1964).

Index